SOCCER IQ

VOLUME 2

MORE OF WHAT SMART PLAYERS DO

DAN BLANK

I invite you to read my blog at www.soccerpoet.com
and to follow me on Twitter: @SoccerPoet

If you would like to place a bulk order of this book in paperback at a
discounted price, please email me at coach@soccerpoet.com.

TABLE OF CONTENTS

INTRODUCTION

"What did I forget? What did I forget?"

That tortured phrase echoed through my head as I deliberated whether or not to push the little button that would officially turn 'Soccer iQ the Word document' into *Soccer iQ* the book. My hand cupped the computer mouse as my index finger tickled the left-click trigger. I stared at the screen for ten minutes, then fifteen, then twenty. This was a big step – huge really – and I didn't want to get it wrong. It was my first book and I wanted to knock it out of the park! I had reached the proverbial point of no return and the one thing I desperately didn't want was to take that leap only to realize a day later that I had left a really great concept out of the text. *Man that would completely stink!*

Well, it didn't take a day. Not even close. Fifteen minutes after *Soccer iQ* was on its way to the printed page, I realized that there was a wonderful chapter that had not occurred to me until it was too late. I jotted it down and labeled it as the first topic of a potential Volume 2. The chapter is called *Plan B,* and you'll be reading it a few pages from now.

With each passing week I'd think of another concept that should have been included in *Soccer iQ* until eventually I had compiled enough of those chapters to justify the release of *Soccer iQ Volume 2*. And here we are.

If you're reading this book, then you've probably also read *Soccer iQ Volume 1.* Thank you for that! Thank you for making it the best-selling soccer book on Amazon! I'm certain that in Mercer County, NJ, many a fine, high school English teacher dropped dead on the spot when they heard the news.

I promised myself that I wouldn't release a *Volume 2* unless I cultivated enough quality content to truly justify its existence. I wasn't going to throw together some rubbish and hope that the second volume would ride the coattails of the first just so I could make a buck. If I was going to put out a sequel, I would only do it with a clear conscience. The question I asked myself was this: *If Volume 1 never existed, would this book be good enough to stand on its own?*

I believe it would.

I hope you'll agree. I hope that by the time you finish, you'll feel that you've gotten *more* than your money's worth.

What I said in the introduction of Volume 1 still holds true: For this book to make a difference, you have to believe that the little things really do matter and that even one of them is enough to win or lose you a game.

Welcome to more of your *Soccer iQ*...

1

MEET YOUR TEAMMATES

Did your whole team buy this book? If so, let me recommend that you all sit down and read this chapter together and then have a quick discussion about how it applies to your team. I guarantee that it will have an immediate and positive impact on your game day performances, and the whole thing shouldn't take you more than 20 minutes.

Soccer passes are not a *one-size-fits-all* proposition. Your team is a collection of individuals. Each player brings to the table a different set of strengths and weaknesses. A simple inventory of those characteristics needs to be applied during the course of a match. It only makes sense that whenever possible, you put your teammates in the best possible situation to be successful. Probably… or at least hopefully, you already try to play to your own strengths; now let's try doing that for your teammates also.

You see Jennifer over there? Yeah, she's great on the ball, but she's no track star. As a matter of fact, she's a little on the slow side. Let's try to keep her out of footraces by playing the ball to her feet. She can do amazing things on the ball, but only if she can get to it.

Ashley on the other hand, well, she can fly! We want her in footraces! If she wants the ball in behind the defense, put it out in front of her and let her run!

Yes, Ashley is lightning fast, but she's also pretty darn short and hasn't won a header in three years. So let's not play the ball to her head unless we have no choice.

Becky however, she's about two inches taller than any of their defenders and she's an excellent header, so when we get into a crossing situation, let's put it up in the air and let her go get it. But if you're going to pass it to her on the ground, make sure you play it to her right foot because her left foot is horrible!

3

And speaking of Becky and her left foot… if Becky is about to cross the ball from the left wing, we know that ball probably won't reach the back post, so we'd better make sure we have at least one runner getting to the near post because that's where the ball is going to land.

Now our right back, Carli, she's a fantastic 1v1 defender, but she doesn't have the world's strongest leg, so there's no point in asking her to hit a 50-yard ball. As a matter of fact, since a lot of her clearances are rather short, our forwards need to drop deeper to help her out when she has to clear the ball.

By now you've probably already started transposing the descriptions of my imaginary players onto your own teammates. Excellent! That's exactly what you should be doing!

If you're in a fantastic position to score a goal, do you want the ball passed to your right foot or your left? You may be so good with either foot that you really don't care, but I assure you, you are part of a very small minority. If you prefer one foot to the other, doesn't it stand to reason that your teammates may feel the same way? Of course it does!

These are the tiny considerations that smart players are constantly making. You know your teammates way better than I do. You've been with them for a while now. You can probably tell me which players are the fastest, the slowest and the best or worst headers. You can probably tell me who is right-footed and who is left-footed. Now, since you know all these things, why not apply that knowledge in the best possible way to give your teammates the best possible chance to be successful and give your team the best possible chance to win?

Years ago I was the assistant coach for a W-League team. The roster was sprinkled with some exceptional Division I college players, but not everyone could make it to our first few training sessions. Going into our first game, some of our players still hadn't even met yet.

As we headed into the stadium, I overheard two of our forwards introducing themselves for the first time. The conversation went like this:

"Hi Jen, I'm Nikki."

"Nice to meet you."

"Where do you want the ball? Do you want it to your feet or in space?"

"I want it at my feet."

"Okay, I'm fast, so play me into space."

That conversation took all of ten seconds, yet it accomplished something very important: it determined what type of pass each player needed so that she could be the most successful. It takes some players half a season to figure that out, but these two got it sorted out ten seconds after they met. Doesn't that make a lot more sense?

Smart players give their teammates the best possible chance to be successful by recognizing their strengths and weaknesses and making the necessary adjustments.

Note for Coaches: Remember that suggestion I made in the first paragraph? Yeah, not kidding. Put your team in a room and have them figure out their teammates' strengths and weaknesses and how they can adjust to them. Your chances for success are much higher when players are maximizing their strengths and accommodating for their weaknesses.

2

PLAN B

Back in my college days, I became a pretty decent pool player and even got good enough to win a couple of eight-ball tournaments. Most pool players evolve the same way: you figure out how to hit the cue ball into another ball in such a way that the latter ball rolls into the pocket. Once you're adept at that, you advance to figuring out how to manipulate the cue ball so it sets up your next shot. At least that's how it went for me. But the real turning point in my improvement came from my composure to back away from a shot I was already in the process of hitting.

Pool is a very mental game. Sometimes you slide the cue stick back and everything seems very quiet and your focus is outstanding and it feels like you exist in a wonderful vacuum. That's when you make shots. But other times, as you pull back on that cue, from out of nowhere the voices in your head start shouting all types of ridiculous things and just before you move your cue into its forward motion, you absolutely know you're going to miss. You know that shot has no chance of success whatsoever. So what do you do? Well, you shoot anyway. And you miss.

The biggest favor I ever did myself as a pool player was to develop the composure to recognize when those voices were about to ruin my shot and then step away from the table. I'd take a deep breath, collect myself and reset my focus. Then my chances of making that shot improved dramatically. Trust me, it's a lot easier said than done.

What's that got to do with soccer? Glad you asked. This is important, so pay attention.

I've had the chance to work with and study a lot of very good players. This chapter is about one of the most important things I've learned. When the difference in technical ability and athleticism between two players is more or less negligible, the composure to change plans on the fly is often what makes one of those players better than the other. Let me explain.

You're about to receive the ball and you've already figured out where your next pass is going to go, and by George, it's going to be a beauty! The pass you're going to play is going to spring a teammate in behind the defense and set up an incredible scoring chance. All you have to do is take a touch to prep the ball, and then you'll play that amazing killer pass. Unfortunately, your first touch is off by just a hair – just enough to give the opponent time to close the seam where you intended to play that pass. What do you do?

Well, based on what I've seen, you try to force that ball into a seam that no longer exists. You refuse to accept the reality of your new situation. Instead you cling to the dream of what used to be and play a pass that, deep down, you know won't work. The result is always the same: the other team takes the ball.

As badly as you want that killer ball to still be on, wishing won't make it so. As phenomenal as your original idea was, you've got to quickly make peace with the fact that the play is no longer available, and then start shopping for other options.

One of the separating factors between a great player and everyone else is the willingness to accept that the phenomenal opportunity that was begging for you a half-second ago is no longer realistic, and then the composure to not force the issue. When Plan A falls apart, it's time to cut your losses and improvise a Plan B.

The crux of Charles Darwin's theory of evolution rests in a species' ability to adapt to a changing environment. Those who fail to adapt, perish. Those who adapt will survive and thrive. It's no different in soccer. The best players are the ones who can adapt to a rapidly changing environment.

In the opening example we discussed a passing opportunity, but this is equally common with shooting chances. Perhaps you're positioned in the penalty box thinking that if that ball comes your way, you're going to hit a first time shot and you're going to score an easy goal. But then the ball arrives a half step behind you, or it takes a bobble just before it reaches you, so you're forced to take a touch to control it. Everyone on the planet knows that the opportunity just isn't there anymore – including you. But the vast majority of players will momentarily suspend rational thought and shoot anyway; and then the shot goes horribly off target or gets blocked by the closing defender.

When you have the ball in the opponent's 18, you're very close to the Promised Land. The last thing you want to do is let the opponent off the hook by shanking the ball out of bounds in a momentary fit of whimsy. And you certainly don't want to take a shot that you know will be blocked by a cavalcade of charging defenders. As badly as you want the glory of being the hero, you've still got to have the composure to exist in the real world. If your shot has no realistic chance of scoring or even reaching the goal, don't ruin your team's territorial advantage by living in denial. Find a teammate who is in a better position to capitalize and get the ball to her. If you have a legitimate chance or even a legitimate half-chance, by all means, pull the trigger. But have the composure to know the difference and act accordingly.

The soccer field is a fluid environment; the picture is always changing and changing quickly; the pieces exist in a constant state of flux. The composure to recognize that an idea has turned sour, *and the willingness to adjust and find a Plan B*, is the bridge between a very good player and a truly great one. Great soccer players are evaluating their decision right up to the moment when their foot hits the ball, and they are perfectly prepared to scrap Plan A if it's no longer realistic, regardless of how great Plan A would have been.

Note for Coaches: Composure is one of soccer's critical intangibles. Players who lack it are going to spend a lot of time donating the ball back to your opponent. Emphasize composure during training sessions. Small-sided games and possession exercises like '31' (as explained in Chapter 8 of *Soccer iQ Vol. 1*) are excellent arenas to address the need to occasionally move on to Plan B.

3

MAGIC NUMBERS

Every team sport has exactly one thing in common. It doesn't matter if it's played indoors or outdoors; on grass, hardwood or clay; on land or in water; it doesn't matter if you play with a ball, puck or shuttlecock: both teams start with an equal number of players. Even teams, at least numerically, are the very foundation of fairness in the world of competition. It's been that way since the beginning and it will be that way until the end of time. When the game begins, your team has the same number of players as my team.

In *Soccer iQ Volume 1*, I proposed that speed of play is the most important thing in soccer, and I stand by that. Sort of. Speed of play is critical for what it creates: possession, a fatigued opponent, etc. But the real prize that can be created by a high tempo is a numerical advantage. So in a chicken and egg sort of way, let me say that numbers are *also* the most important thing in soccer. And the most important numbers of all are 2v1. Those are the magic numbers.

Let's begin with a simple truism about soccer numbers: Lower numbers favor the attacking team; higher numbers favor the defending team. For the team that has the ball, a 1v1 is better than a 2v2, which is better than a 3v3 or 6v6 or 10v10. On the other hand, the team without the ball is better off playing 6v8 than 2v2. A crowd favors the defending team. That's why, when a team has the chance to attack 2v2, it should make every effort to keep that attack going forward at maximum speed. As the opponent is sprinting back to recover, a 2v2 can and will turn into a 7v7 very quickly. Still with me?

The next thing to consider is that there is no bigger advantage in team sports than a numerical advantage. Think back to when you were just a kid and teams were being chosen on the playground. Wasn't it important to start with an even number so you would end up with even teams? And what did you do when there was an odd number? You had to make some type of accommodation so neither team enjoyed a numerical advantage. You may have even made the odd kid sit out until someone else showed up, or maybe you played with a 'steady' quarterback or pitcher. Regardless, you found a way to make the teams numerically even.

One extra player makes a big, big difference in team sports. That's why there's a penalty in the NFL if a team lines up with an extra man on the field, and why the crowd will rise to its feet for a 2 on 1 break in basketball, and why we *hate* seeing a teammate being given a red card but quietly celebrate if that red card is given to one of our opponents. A numerical advantage of one can be a game-changer.

To illustrate further, let's look at hockey. I'm a big NHL fan and I'm fascinated by the parallels between hockey and soccer. To me, hockey looks a lot like 6v6 soccer, except it's played on ice by guys with sticks who occasionally beat the snot out of one another.

One of the things I love about hockey is its penal system, also known as the power play. When a player from one team commits a foul, he sits in the penalty box for two minutes and his team plays down a man. Why is this a big deal? Because one team gets to play with an extra player! And why is that a big deal? Because roughly one-fourth of all goals scored in the NHL come on the power play. In a sport that resembles soccer, this statistic demonstrates the value of an extra player.

Hopefully I've convinced you of the value of the numerical advantage. Now it's up to you to figure out how to create as many of them as possible during the course of a match.

One of the great challenges to any soccer team is to create a numerical advantage when there is none. A team that does this well is going to win a lot of games. And the magic number that you should be looking for is a 2v1.

There is no more important numerical combination in soccer than a 2v1. Why? Because a 2v1 can quickly turn into a 1v0. 2v1s can be created anywhere on the field. But finding them can be a bit like the brain-teaser game where you have to find a small picture hidden within a bigger picture. Smart soccer players can assess a picture of many pieces and then find that smaller picture.

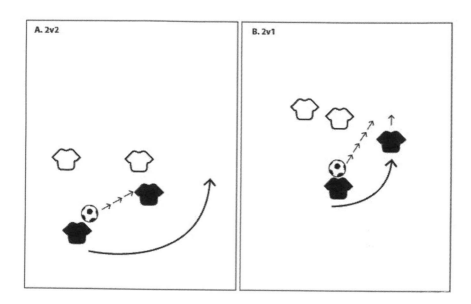

I don't know that a book can teach you how to recognize opportunities to create 2v1s, but the diagram demonstrates how an overlapping run can turn a 2v2 into a 2v1. If the overlap is executed successfully, both defenders are eliminated and the 2v1 becomes a 1v0... at least for the time being.

There are many ways to extract 2v1s from the bigger numerical picture. As a smart soccer player you need to search for these opportunities, recognize and exploit them. These are the moments that will win you games.

Note for Coaches: A good way to introduce this concept to your players is through small-sided, grid games like 2v2, 3v3 and 4v4 where the objective is to stop the ball on your opponent's endline. Adding a neutral player will make it easier to create these situations, but eventually the players need to figure out how to convert even numbers into a numerical advantage during the run of play.

4

THE FISHHOOK RUN

One of the most effective ways to exploit a 2v1 is with a fishhook run, also known as a 'square and through' run or a 'J' run.

In this diagram below, we have a 2v1 developing near the sideline.

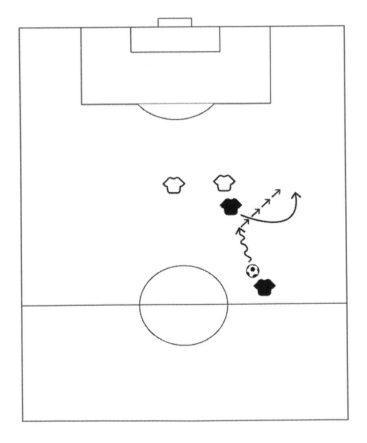

In this situation, the defender will have no choice but to stay tucked inside to confront the ball-carrier. Attacker #2 now has three jobs:

Job 1 is to create a seam wide enough for Attacker #1 to play a penetrating pass that eliminates the defender.

Job 2 is to stay onside.

Job 3 is to hit the offside line at full speed.

So how does she do it? Simple. She uses the fishhook run.

As soon as the higher attacker realizes that the opponent who is marking her is preparing to confront the ball, she immediately peels out toward the sideline. Since the defender must stay inside to confront the ball, this run opens up a seam between that defender and the sideline. The attacker must focus on getting wide enough to open a clear seam so that the defender can't stick a foot out to deflect the pass.

The most common mistake players make here is cutting off the run too soon, which leaves the ball-carrier with a seam that isn't wide enough to play a penetrating pass. The ball-carrier either plays a pass that gets blocked, or she adjusts and plays a ball that is too square to eliminate the defender. Either way, the opportunity to exploit the 2v1 is lost. Remember, when you're the player making that fishhook run, you don't want to merely receive the ball; you want to receive the ball in such a way that the defender is eliminated.

As the higher attacker peels out wide, she should also bend her run slightly back toward her own goal. Bending the run like this will ensure that she stays onside if the defender charges forward. It also gives her the chance to build up a step or two of forward momentum when she turns forward and hits the offside line.

Incidentally, when you are making this run, do it at a full sprint and remember to look over your shoulder to see what's happening on the ball.

If you do all of this correctly, the ball-carrier is left with a comfortable seam to push the ball beyond the frozen defender and the defender is subsequently eliminated. You've successfully exploited a 2v1! Congratulations!

Note for Coaches: Your team is going to struggle to win games if it can't recognize and exploit 2v1 situations. There are plenty of simple exercises to train the fishhook run. The diagram below gives you a way to work this run into a crossing exercise. Use a passive/stationary defender to confront the ball. Add defenders to challenge the crosses.

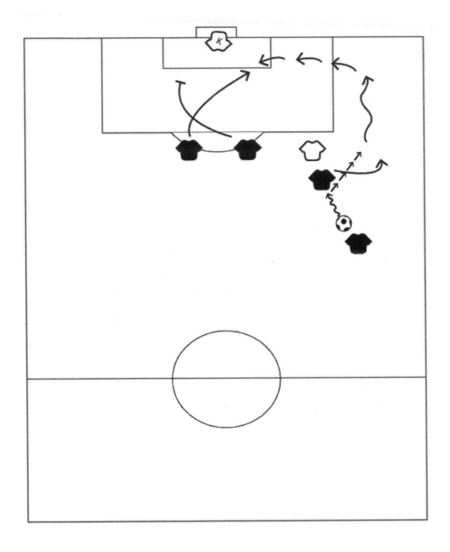

5

PLAY BEHIND THE FENCE

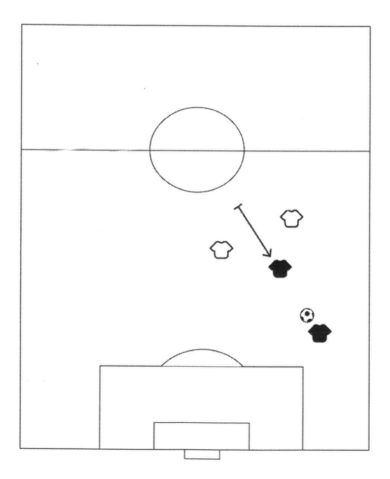

Let's say that you are the central player in the above diagram. You've moved between – and in front of – two opponents to offer support for your teammate on the ball. The problem is that when you receive that pass, you are in front of those two opponents and they've seen the whole play develop, so it is easy for them to quickly close in on you. This will make it almost impossible for you to turn. It will make it very difficult for you to do anything other than to pass the ball back to the teammate who initially passed it to you. We can do better than that, and it's a really simple fix.

Imagine that a fence runs between those two opponents. When you receive it in front of them, you are fenced in. But if you stay behind them and behind their line of vision, the ball can get to you outside of that fence. If you receive it behind the fence, you've got an excellent chance of breaking pressure. You will be in a much better position to turn and you will have many more options once you do.

Remember, soccer has a bit of hide-and-seek in it. It's the defender's job to find you. It's not your job to jump in front of them and say, *"Hey Everybody! Here I am!"* You need to be a little sneakier than that. If you can receive the ball behind the fence, your life is a lot easier.

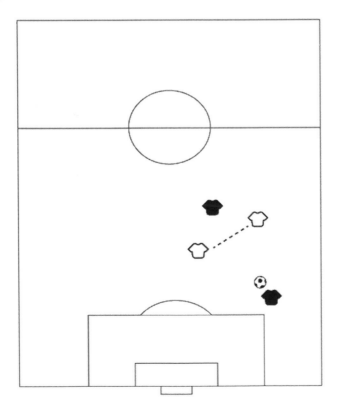

In this diagram, the fence is represented by the dashed line. The supporting player stays behind the fence and is in a much better position to turn when she receives the ball.

Note for Coaches: This is a principle that all players need to understand, but it is particularly crucial for your central midfielders. They are the players who link your backs to your forwards and your left side to your right. They are the ones who often determine whether or not your team breaks pressure. They need to put themselves in the best possible position to turn the ball.

6

SKIP A LAYER

For this chapter to make sense, you'll need to think of your team in layers. Your goalkeeper is a layer, then your defenders, then your defensive midfielders, then your attacking midfielders and then your forwards. Those are your vertical layers. Your horizontal layers are your right-sided players, your right-sided central players, your left-sided central players and your left-sided players.

I've always been big on possession-based, indirect soccer. My training sessions are always heavy on possession exercises and as I mentioned in Volume 1, there can be a danger in that because players will become conditioned to play their way out of everything with short passes and their vision starts to max out at 15 or 20 yards. Well, short passes aren't always the best option and they can get you into trouble really quickly if you don't know when it's time to play big.

The soccer ball is a magnet. Players are drawn to it and that's why it doesn't take very long for a crowd to form around it. A smart player will recognize when a crowd is converging around her and when a short pass, even one that will reach the intended teammate, is just a way to ensure that the other team takes the ball. When it's gotten too tight, a smart player knows to skip a layer. Here's a simple example: A team can switch a ball through its defenders by having the right back play to the right-center back, who plays to the left center back, who plays to the left back. But, as illustrated in the diagram, when the right back plays directly to the left-center back, she's skipped the right-center back. In effect, she's skipped a layer. If the left-center back then passes directly into a forward, she's bypassed the midfield, and again a layer has been skipped.

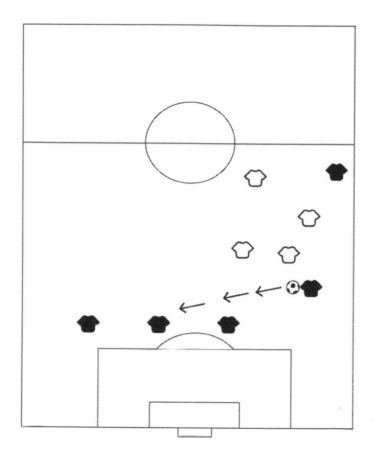

No matter how many possession exercises your team does, your vision has got to be greater than 15 yards, and you've got to recognize when things are getting crowded. In situations where the opponent is getting a lot of numbers around the ball, be prepared to play a bigger pass.

Note for Coaches: If you always train in small areas, your players will become conditioned to look almost exclusively for short options. Mix possession exercises into your training that incorporate large sections of the field to challenge players to expand their fields of vision. Players need to understand that there's a real value to a 40-yard ball that solves pressure by eliminating a large number of opponents.

7

THE HIGHER OF TWO OPTIONS

This one fits in nicely with the 'skip a layer' theme from the previous chapter. This is good common sense for all soccer players, but defenders really need to pay attention to this one. Forgive me for the oversimplified math.

If you are looking to play a forward pass and you can successfully deliver it to your closest teammate who is ten yards in front of you, or you can successfully deliver that pass to a teammate ten yards farther up the field, play the bigger pass. Here's why…

If you play the ball to the closest teammate and she has to play the way she is facing, you might be her only passing option. You play a ten-yard pass to her and she plays a ten-yard pass right back to you, you've gained no ground. In effect, it was a zero sum transaction. However, if you play the twenty yard pass and the teammate who receives it plays the way she is facing, the bypassed teammate is already underneath the target and immediately becomes an option to receive that next ball. So you play a 20-yard forward pass and your target plays a ten-yard negative pass, well then you've gained ten yards and the final player in that puzzle is facing the direction your team wants to go. Follow me, there?

The ball is like a magnet, especially for opposing players, and they are going to gravitate toward the ball. So, beyond the simple territorial gain, the longer pass is more likely to break the opponent's pressure and the recipient of the longer pass is more likely to have a wider variety of options upon receiving the ball. These are good things.

This is a common issue for teams that play with two levels of midfielders, such as an attacking center mid and a defensive center mid. When a defender has possession of the ball, the defensive center mid is often the closest and therefore easiest option, so we tend to give her the ball. But if we can stretch our vision another fifteen yards up the field, we may find a clear path into the attacking center mid. If we can get her the ball, then the defensive center mid becomes an option for that next pass.

The diagram illustrates a typical situation where the longer pass eliminates more opponents and gives the target a built-in passing option underneath her.

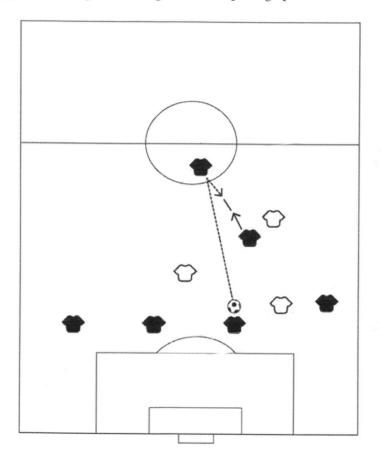

Note for Coaches: When it comes to instituting the pattern in the diagram, the key is making sure the lower player doesn't get directly between the ball and the higher target. If she moves onto that line, she clogs the ball's path to the higher player and eliminates her as an option. At that point the lower player is, in effect, playing for the other team. If she starts to clog that seam, the higher player has to tell her to get out.

If you play a lot of possession games at training, particularly ones with direction, you'll have ample opportunities to observe this situation and make corrections. Here's one of my favorite possession games and it will help you point out those moments when playing to the higher player is the better option. And if you read the first volume of *Soccer iQ*, you'll also get to make many wonderful corrections about supporting "better than square."

The Four-Target Game

The field is 45 x 25 yards. Each team puts five players in the grid and one target off each end of the field. You may want to start with a neutral player as well. The targets may not defend one another. Players cannot leave the grid to defend the targets. Targets may not enter the field to receive the ball. Targets start with a two-touch restriction and may not play directly to one another. Rotate targets every two minutes. There is no offside.

The object is to get the ball in to one target and receive the return pass, then get the ball into the other target and again receive the return pass, without losing the ball along the way. In short, a team scores by delivering the ball into both targets without conceding possession. You can play into the same target two or more times in succession, but you only score by getting it to both targets. If you get the ball into one target, lose possession, then regain possession, you can attack to either target.

This game gives you lots of options. Here are a few I like:
- The targets are restricted to one touch
- Field players are restricted to one or two touches
- The target cannot return the ball to the teammate who passed it to her
- The pass into the target must come from behind midfield
- When the target receives the ball, she immediately comes onto the field and a teammate must immediately replace her

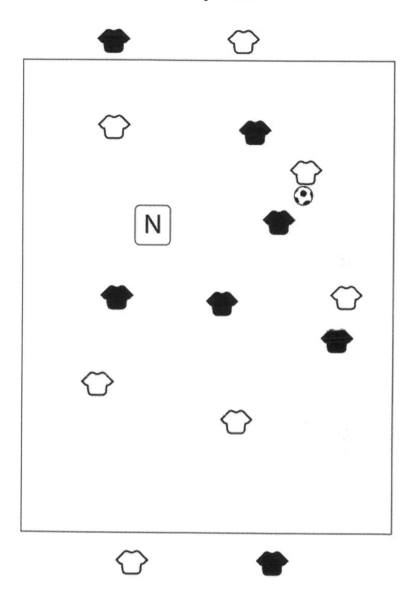

8

PLAY IT TO WHERE SHE'S GOING, NOT WHERE SHE'S AT

The title of this chapter is pretty self-explanatory.

This chapter applies most commonly to a situation in which we are trying to play a ball in to a forward who is making either a lateral run across the line of defenders or a diagonal run beyond it. Either way, this pass often fails because you angle your pass back into her run instead of playing it in front of her.

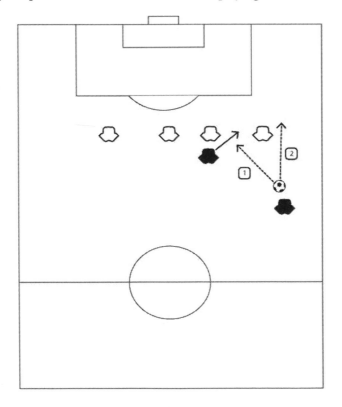

In this diagram, the center forward is looking for a seam ball between Defender 4 and the sideline, but entry pass #1 is angled between Defenders 3 and 4.

Typically this pass ends up a few steps behind the forward, missing her completely. Even if you are *successful* in getting the pass to the target's body, it is an extremely difficult ball for her to receive, as her momentum is taking her in the opposite direction. Now she is forced to quickly stop, open her hips and receive the ball with her trailing foot. This is a lot harder than it might sound. And oh by the way, she has to do all of that under pressure from the defender.

So how do we fix this? Simple.

First we have to accept the fact that we are passing to a moving target. Where that target is now is not where she will be even a half second from now. So we have to do a quick calculation in our head by observing how fast she is running and which direction she is headed and then produce a pass that will ideally keep her in stride. Additionally, whenever possible, instead of angling this pass back against her momentum, straighten it out and play a pass that is directly vertical. This straight pass will be much easier for your teammate to handle while she's at a full gallop.

In the diagram, entry pass #2 is a better option as it provides the attacker a ball she can run onto. So instead of playing the ball into the seam occupied by the attacker, we play it one seam ahead of her.

Note for Coaches: Chapter 16 of *Soccer iQ Volume 1* includes a diagram of one of my favorite training exercises, the End-Zone Game. This exercise will give you ample opportunities to observe and correct players who play the ball into the wrong seam.

9

TO JUMP OR NOT TO JUMP

Here's one for the defenders.

The other team has played a long, flighted ball that might go over your head. An attacker is steaming down the field, trying to get onto the end of that pass. Your choice is whether to jump and head the ball, or to turn and run toward your own goal.

This situation will often turn into a goal because of a defender who has either misjudged the flight of the ball or misjudged her own leaping ability. The ball either clears the defender on the fly, or the defender inadvertently flicks it onto the pressing attacker. Either way it's bad news for the defending team.

If you can win that ball with your head, by all means you should definitely do that! Go up and head it away! However, when you make that choice, know that you're pushing your chips all in. If you decide to make your stand by going up to head the ball, you've got to be absolutely certain you can win it; because if you don't win it and the ball goes over your head, *you are toast*. By the time you stop, jump, land, and then turn and run, you'll never catch the attacker who has zoomed past you. And by the way, she'll have the ball and be speeding towards your goal.

So, if you're not certain… if there is a lingering doubt about whether you can get enough of your head to that ball, don't waste your time jumping. Instead, turn and run and try to keep your body aligned with the path of the ball. If the ball goes over your head, at least you'll have a fighting chance to win the race to it. And if you are very lucky, the ball may hit the back of your head or your neck or your back. Okay, those may not be the prettiest surface choices, but any one of them is a heckuva lot better than that ball getting past you.

Note for Coaches: I have the luxury of spending a lot of time with our defenders, so yes, this is actually a topic we cover. I urge you to spend a few games watching how many times opponents get behind your defense because someone attempts an ill-advised header. Let your defenders know that there comes a time and a place to just turn and run.

10

NO BLIND NEGATIVE PASSES

Have you ever played by sound? You have the ball at your feet, your head is down, and you hear a teammate screaming for the ball so you pass it in the direction of her voice. Ever done that? Sure you have. We all have. And we've all gotten away with it. And chances are there have been times when we've also not gotten away with it.

An excellent way to start an attack for your opponent is to have one of your negative passes intercepted. The closer you play to your own goal, the more perilous these passes become. You've got to incorporate some risk management into your negative passes and here is a very simple and effective rule of thumb that I use with our defenders: Don't play a negative pass without first looking at your target.

It sounds simple enough, and it is, but it's exceptionally important. I don't want our right back passing to our center back without first looking at her. And I don't want our center back (or anyone else) passing to our goalkeeper without first looking at her. Taking that quick look will give you all the information you need to assess your situation and determine if you should play that back-pass or find an alternative solution, even if it means kicking the ball out of bounds and conceding a throw-in.

Clever forwards are predators. They will bait defenders into dangerous passes and then pounce on them. It's like a game of hide-and-go-score. The best way to protect yourself is to take a quick look up in the direction you wish to play. If an opposing forward is lying in wait, you'll be able to negate her ability to surprise you and you'll save yourself an awful lot of heartache.

When you're passing back to your goalkeeper, there's one more great reason to take a quick look: You want to make sure that you pass the ball to her and not past her. Many an own goal has been scored thanks to an errant pass intended for the 'keeper. Make sure you have some type of visual contact before you pass her that ball. Don't donate a goal to the opponent.

When that pass comes off of your foot, until it arrives at your teammate, it is *your* responsibility. Even when you feel the pressure bearing down on your back, take a quick peak before you pass the ball. If you don't, you are asking for trouble.

Note for Coaches: Negative passes that become turnovers have a nasty habit of becoming goals.

I implore our defenders to take a look before they play a negative pass. The key is convincing them that they actually have the tenth of a second it requires to sneak that peek. You have to stress composure.

11

THE SUICIDE PASS

Here's the situation: You're a wide player, such as the right back, and you have the ball. You decide to play a square pass to the center back.

Your pass may get there or it may not, but understand this: you've just played the suicide pass – the riskiest pass in soccer. And it's not just risky for defenders; it's risky for anyone in any position. Let me tell you why.

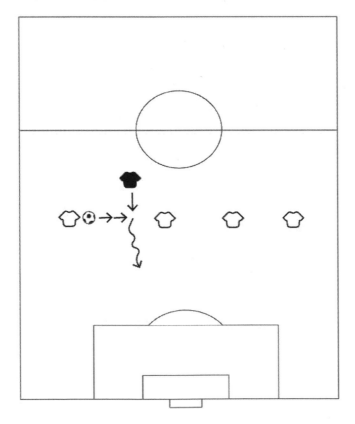

In the first diagram, the defender with the ball has played a square pass to her center back, but the opposing forward is stepping in to intercept it. As soon as the attacker has taken the ball, there's been a nasty change in the numerical balance of the field. Simply put, there's been a three-person swing. The two defenders are subtracted from the equation (-2) and the attacker who is now in behind both of them has been added to the equation (+1). When a three-person swing happens that suddenly, bad things happen.

Keep in mind that at the moment of possession change, the attacker is already moving and the two defenders are more likely to be stationary – particularly the one who is waiting to receive the ball. When the race starts, the defenders are immediately at a tremendous disadvantage. The outside back who made the initial pass will be caught wide of the ball and will have no real chance to recover and affect play. The center back's odds are only slightly better, depending on how high up the field this all took place and how fast she can run.

All square balls are dangerous for exactly this reason, but when the pass is played from a wider position to a more central one, the turnovers tend to be much less forgiving. In the next diagram, because the pass has been played from a central position to a wider one, the passer may have the chance to read the pending interception and begin a recovery run that will put her between the ball and the goal. You might get away with this one. But when the intercepted square pass comes from the outside in, there's no two ways around it, your team is in trouble.

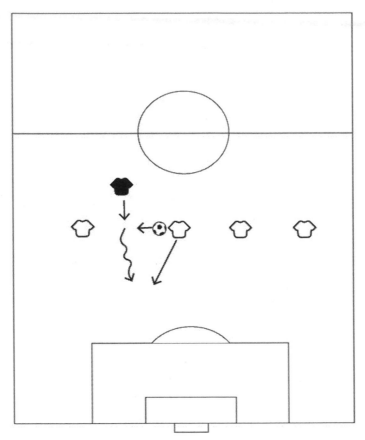

We've specifically addressed defenders because that's when the consequences of a botched suicide pass can be the most glaring and immediate and turn into clear cut breakaways. But the suicide pass is dangerous for all of your teammates, particularly when they are playing in your half of the field. Let's say that your team has possession of the ball, 45 yards up the field, and before the ball is ever passed, the numerical situation is 6v5 in your favor. The instant that ball is picked off, those numbers change to 4v6 against you and the opponent is steaming right toward your goal. That's a great time to be your opponent.

In the last chapter I advised you to never play a blind, negative ball. The same rule applies here. Before you play that square pass, get a visual and make sure that there's no chance of that ball being intercepted.

Note for Coaches: Have you ever heard that soccer games are lost more than they are won? The suicide pass is a wonderful crystallization of this concept. This is a mistake that tends to get punished on the scoreboard, so make your players aware of the risks involved when playing a square pass toward the center of the park.

12

CHOOSE YOUR BATTLES

Here's a chapter for all of you compulsive dribblers who want to showcase your dribbling brilliance every time the ball finds your feet. Let's start with the good news; if dribbling is your addiction, then chances are you're pretty good at it. If you're not sure, ask your coach. If he tells you otherwise, then my advice is to dribble less and pass more and move on to the next chapter. However, if you are a genuinely talented dribbler, then we need to talk.

There is a difference between being a talented dribbler and being an effective one, and being one doesn't guarantee that you are automatically the other. The talented dribbler is technical and fluid and superb with her change of direction. There is no implied result to what she does, only that it's pretty to watch. The talented dribbler can be either effective or ineffective.

The effective dribbler makes things happen. There is a purpose to her dribbling and that purpose is to get past her opponent as quickly as possible to create a numerical advantage going forward and to create goal-scoring opportunities.

If you're a talented dribbler, you should strive to become an effective one. Follow me?

Years ago I coached one of the best dribblers in college soccer. As you might expect, she wanted to solve every situation by dribbling through it. Why? Because she was immensely talented. The girl could tie opponents in knots. She could change directions so quickly and so often that defenders would practically screw themselves into the ground. The problem was that many times when she was engaged in her 1v1 extravaganzas, she wasn't necessarily going anywhere. And the ball certainly wasn't going anywhere either. And neither was our attack. As she toyed with an opponent, all of the opponent's teammates were getting back behind the ball and getting organized. So while our player was slowly winning her individual battle, we were losing the bigger war. Her dribbling would often do us more harm than good because it cost us our numerical advantages.

Every dribbling duel is a battle, and every battle takes time. When your team is launching an attack, time is the enemy. The longer your individual battle lasts, the more time your opponent has to get bodies behind the ball and get organized. When your immediate objective is to dribble past an opponent, the faster you can get the job done, the better off your team will be. And isn't that the important part?

To be an effective dribbler, you need to understand how your dribbling fits into the big picture. You need to understand when and where passing is a better alternative than dribbling, even if you ultimately go on to win your dribbling duel. Dribbling isn't the objective; dribbling to create chances is. If your dribbling is slowing down the attack, you're costing your team chances.

To be an effective dribbler, you've got to choose your battles. If your team can attack faster if you pass instead of dribble, then pass. Advancing the ball 30 yards up the field with a pass is a heckuva lot faster than advancing the ball 30 yards on the dribble. Remember that.

Since we are on the topic of choosing your battles, let me say that if you are facing your own goal and there is pressure on your back and you have support underneath you, this could be the ideal time to showcase your unselfish nature and select your passing option *early*. One of my great pet peeves is when a player who is in this situation tries two or three dribbling forays before realizing that the situation is unwinnable, *and then* decides to lay the ball back to a teammate. If you're going to pass the ball back to her anyway, can you just do it early and get it over with? The longer you wait to pass that ball, the more difficult you make life for the teammate who is about to receive it and the more time you give the opponent to get organized. Your teammate is already facing the direction you ultimately want to go, so there's an excellent chance she already has the problem solved, so would you *JUST PASS HER THE DARN BALL!*

As a general rule of thumb, you may want to make some of these 'dribble or pass' decisions based on the area of the field in which you receive the ball. A lot of coaches prefer that you first look to pass when you are in the defensive and middle thirds of the field, and then showcase your dribbling in the attacking third. Beating a defender 1v1 in the final third will often lead directly to a cross or a shot or some other type of scoring opportunity. On the other hand, if you beat an opponent on the dribble on your side of the center circle, you still have 70 yards to go before you get to the goal. Remember, it's all about the big picture.

Note for Coaches: I've coached several players with this ailment and every one of them grew up training in an environment that emphasized fast footwork patterns. These players got really good at those patterns and loved showcasing their ability to change directions. But too often, they couldn't see the forest for their trees. To address this issue with the player mentioned above, we explained how her dribbling expeditions were slowing down our attack and that we didn't need to see every tool in her toolbox every time she got the ball. Then we asked her to start choosing her battles more carefully. When she started doing that, she became a much more effective player.

1 3

AIM SMALL, MISS SMALL

I recently improvised a little experiment with five of my college players. They came out before training to get in some extra shooting practice, so I decided we would work on hitting side-volleys. They stood in a line, ten yards in front of the goal. I was kneeling about four yards away from them with all the soccer balls. I would gently toss them a ball that came in about waist-high, and they would try to smack it into the goal. There were 40 balls, so each player took eight shots. At the end of the round, about half of the balls were in the goal; the other half had flown over or wide of it.

I changed up the exercise for the second round by placing a wooden bench on the center of the goal line. Now their objective was to hit the bench with their side-volleys. At the end of the round, the bench had been hit eight or nine times. Not great, right? Well consider this... of those 40 shots that were struck in round two, only one ended up going over the goal. The other 39 were in the net. That's a pretty remarkable improvement by anyone's standards.

When the players had the whole goal to shoot at, they weren't selective about the specific spot in the goal where they wanted to deliver the ball. They were technically undisciplined and therefore they weren't very accurate. But as soon as they had to focus on a much smaller target, suddenly they couldn't miss the net!

I'm a big proponent of leaving yourself as much margin for error as possible, particularly when it comes to shooting. You can miss wide of the goal, and you can miss over the goal, but it is physically impossible to miss under the goal.

The whole goal gives shooters a target area of 192 square feet. The wooden bench (six feet long x 1.5 feet high) gave my players a target area of 9 square feet. Naturally they missed it much more often than they hit it, but focusing on the smaller target gave them much more margin for error. Even when they were missing the bench, they were still scoring goals.

When you are close to the goal and the ball you're about to shoot is off the ground, aim for the goal line. Try to drive that ball in such a way that it literally skips off the goal line on its way to the net. When you aim small like this, you're leaving yourself about 7.5 feet of margin for error. In a goal that's eight feet high, that's a pretty good cushion. I mean, you could miss your target by seven feet and still score!

When you aim small, you are less likely to be sloppy with your technique. You are more likely to be focused and to shorten your leg swing. What does that mean? You're more likely to score. And isn't that a good thing?

Note for Coaches: I often put a small target, like that bench, on the goal line when I run shooting sessions for all the reasons you just read. It's amazing how much more focused players are when they have a smaller target to work with. We even built a 3' x 24' portable goal, which is excellent for working on striking a ball that is rolling back toward the shooter. That particular shot is one that players will regularly send to the moon, so the smaller target forces them to shorten their swing and focus on making technically sound contact with the ball.

14

I HATE THIS RUN AND YOU SHOULD TOO

Let's say you're the center forward. Your winger has the ball on the flank and has just entered the attacking third. She's faced up the opponent's outside back and is prepared to go at her in a 1v1 duel. What do you do?

Well, here's what too many of you do too often: As indicated in the diagram, you make a diagonal run to the corner, dragging a defender along with you. Now that 1v1 battle has become a little too crowded and the teammate on the ball has to find a new plan. This is an excellent way to take a promising attack and grind it to a screeching halt.

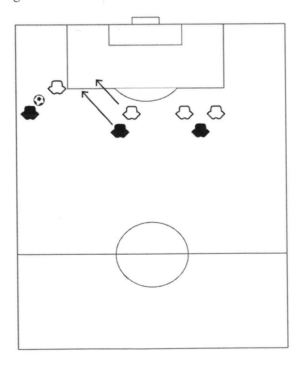

Let's begin with the small problem. If your winger plays you that pass up the sideline, there's only one way for you to receive it, and that's pinned against the sideline with your back to the field (and all of your teammates) and a defender breathing down your neck. On your best day you might turn this into a corner kick. More often than not it ends up as a throw-in, and often for the other team. There is typically very little to gain from this run.

Here's the bigger problem: you've totally ruined that 1v1 situation for your winger. She had that defender out on an island. Your winger was faced up against a defender who had no help, and then you went and brought the help to her. Look, 1v1 is a phenomenal attacking equation. If your winger is a good 1v1 attacker, then just stay the heck out of her way and let her do her job. If the opponent isn't going to provide cover for the outside back, don't force them into it. Just leave your teammate alone to do her job and go get in front of the goal and await her cross.

Note for Coaches: Some coaches will wholeheartedly disagree with me on this one and that's fine, but I'm always happy to see opponents making this run. As far as I'm concerned, they can attack the corner flags all they want. The reason players make this run is because the seam between the outside back and the sideline is the easiest one to get into and receive the ball. But it's the easiest because it is also the least dangerous and least problematic to defend. If you take my side on this one, here's how to fix it: Draw it up on the board. Then go on the field and walk your players through it. Then yell at your center forward when she makes this run anyway.

15

HANDS DOWN DEFENDING

When you are attempting to block a shot or a cross, keep your hands down at your sides; and whenever possible, put your hands behind your back. In these situations, the ball has a nasty habit of finding its way into an outstretched arm, and the result is often a hand ball. Obviously this becomes even more critical when you are standing inside your own penalty box, as these handballs typically turn into penalty kicks which subsequently turn into goals.

And oh by the way, I've seen many examples where an attacker crossed a ball from the edge of the 18 that caromed off something other than the defender's outstretched arm, only to be whistled as a penalty kick anyway. Twice I've seen penalty kicks called when a cross smacked the defender square in the face! Those movements happen so fast that it's easy for an official to be deceived, especially if your arms are flailing away from your body. Keeping your arms down and your hands behind your back is a wonderful insurance policy. It makes it virtually impossible for the referee to award a penalty kick for a phantom foul.

Now, this is a lot easier said than done, for two reasons. The natural motion of your body will frequently leave you with a raised arm, so you have to make a conscious effort to keep your arms down. It's not easy, but it's definitely doable. The key is recognizing that you are about to be in a shot-blocking or cross-blocking situation before the ball is ever struck, and then making the decision to keep your arms down.

Body control is actually the easier of the two challenges faced by shot-blockers and cross-blockers. The real challenge is exhibiting good, old-fashioned courage. It takes a something a little bit special to stand there with your arms at your side when an opponent is about to lace a guided missile in your direction. Doesn't matter. Do it anyway. Have the courage to stand in front of that ball like you're about to take a bullet for the President. Make a conscious choice to be brave. If that ball hits you, yes, it's going to hurt a little bit. Heck, it may hurt a lot. But you know what, ten seconds later it won't hurt anymore and you'll be carrying on with your game. However, if you put your hands up to protect yourself and that ball strikes your arm, you've just gifted the opponent a goal. Choose courage. It's the better option.

Note for Coaches: There is a craft to shot-blocking that goes beyond mere courage. Shot-blocking is a skill and you can teach your players to improve at it. However, it won't matter if they don't have the bravery to go with it. I treat our shot-blockers like heroes! I absolutely love them! Anytime one of our players blocks a shot or a cross, I enthusiastically celebrate her courage in front of her teammates. Teams don't win without courageous players. Sometimes you just have to muster up two seconds of courage, because that's what heroes do.

16

GOOD THEATER

There are three balls and one strike on the batter. The next pitch is on the outside edge of the strike zone. The batter immediately begins to trot toward first base because the pitcher just threw ball four. Or did he? The umpire hasn't yet made the call. So why did the batter start toward first base before the umpire ruled ball four? Because he's trying to convince the umpire that the pitch was clearly not a strike. Yes, there is theater in all sports, and soccer is no exception.

As much as no one wants to say it out loud, part of being a smart soccer player is being a good actor. Referees are only human and they can't always see exactly what happened, so often times their calls are influenced by the immediate reactions of the players around the ball. You need to digest this knowledge and apply it regularly.

Let's begin by saying that anytime the ball goes out of bounds and should be legitimately awarded to your team, emphasize the fact by pointing in the direction you are attacking and saying something like, "Red ball!" or "Corner!" Now in theory you shouldn't have to do this, but you need to anyway. Why? Because if you don't say, "Corner!" but a player on the other team shouts, "Goal kick!," the referee may be swayed to award the goal kick. Face it… it happens. A lot.

Occasionally you'll encounter a team that has been coached to campaign for every single throw-in, even when the ball should clearly go to the opponent. Every time the ball goes out of bounds they have fifteen people shouting, "Red ball!" What makes these teams more annoying than their incessant whining is the fact that occasionally their whining gets rewarded because the referee just didn't see what happened. I don't think you should campaign for a ball unless it should legitimately be your ball or the action happened so fast that it would be difficult for an official to make a clear judgment. If you think the officials might have trouble making the call along the sideline, go ahead and try to steal the throw-in.

If you're going to try to steal a throw-in, you've got to act like that ball belongs to you beyond a shadow of a doubt and anyone who thinks otherwise is an idiot. You've got to be convincing and you've got to be quick. You have to be BOTH. A lot of players come very close to stealing a throw-in. A player will pick the ball up right away and cock it behind her head and everyone has every reason to believe that ball belongs to her. She's about a half-second away from committing the perfect crime because so far she's been very convincing. But then she can't bring herself to actually throw the ball back onto the field without first pausing to look at the referee to see if she's actually going to get away with it. And at that moment of slight hesitation, the jig is up. The referee is given an extra second to replay the scene in his head and then he sees the guilt in your eyes and that's all he needs to blow his whistle and give the other team the ball. If you're going to try to steal a throw-in, put the ball back in play in a hurry. The referee is a lot less likely to halt the play once the ball is back on the field.

Handballs are another instance when some good acting may save your team. When that ball suddenly hits you in the arm, the referee will either make the call or he won't. It's not your job to confess, particularly not in your own penalty box. The best piece of advice I can give you is to keep playing, *without the slightest hesitation*, as if the ball never touched your arm — as if you don't even have arms! It's a difficult decision for a referee to whistle a penalty kick. When you pause after that ball hits your arm, even for just split second, you're inviting the ref to blow the whistle. And if by chance the ball smashes into your forearm with enough force to sting you, for the love of Pete, please don't rub it — at least not until it's too late for the referee to blow his whistle. Just act like it never happened. The pain in your arm will quickly subside. The pain of that penalty kick may linger on for much longer.

Note for Coaches: An out-of-bounds restart can be a lot like a Lost and Found item - the first person to claim it, gets it. Claiming restarts, particularly the ones that should legitimately belong to your team, is a pretty important topic. Think of it this way: Do you want your corner kick to become the opponent's goal kick?

When we play small-sided games and the ball goes out of bounds, if the team that the ball should belong to doesn't *claim* the ball but the opponent does, I'll let the opponent keep the restart. Then, someone on the first team will wake up and say, *"Wait, that should be our ball!"*

I'll tell her and her teammates, *"Too bad. You should have said something when it went over the line."*

I've said it before and I'll say it again: You're not running a charity. You've got to compete for your restarts.

17

GET SOMETHING

When you are pinned up against a sideline or an end-line and your chance of producing anything worthwhile is about to vanish, do me a favor and *get something!*

Yes, I know you would much rather send in a beautiful cross for your friend to volley into the side-netting, but when any realistic prospect of that actually happening has disappeared, go to Plan B and win us a throw-in or a corner kick. How? Simple. Just whack the ball off the opponent's shin and then try to avoid the deflection that comes off her leg. There are clever forwards who will bait defenders into following them to the end-line simply so they can bounce the ball off of them to win a corner kick.

Yeah, I know there's not a lot of glory in throw-ins, but at least your team gets to keep the ball and there's nothing wrong with that. And if you win a corner, that's even better.

While we're at it, let's flip this one around. Let's say you're pressuring an opponent near the sideline, and she's off-balance and facing her own goal and is attempting to spin and clear a ball up the sideline, you have to make a quick analysis of her chances to realistically keep that clearance in bounds. If her odds are not good, try to get out of the way.

We often see outside backs in this situation and frequently, the clearance that would have sailed straight out of bounds ends up ricocheting off the pressuring forward and the defender ends up winning the throw-in. If she's going to give you a throw-in, jump out of her way. Remember, something is better than nothing, so *get something!*

Note for Coaches: There is a certain craft to winning restarts and it doesn't happen by accident. This is one of those sub-topics that you can weave into your coaching during possession exercises and small-sided games.

18

THE TRANSITION THROW-IN

You and an opponent are battling against the sideline when the ball pops out of bounds. You quickly scoop it up with the intention of throwing it in. The opponent thinks it's her ball so she's also standing out of bounds trying to obstruct you from taking your throw-in. The referee signals that he's awarded the throw-in to the opponent. What do you do?

Well, first and foremost, *don't hand her the darn ball* because she's just going to throw it in while you're caught out of position. Secondly, don't throw the ball 15 yards down the field or do some other foolish thing that will earn you a yellow card.

Want a really simple way to delay this throw-in without putting yourself in the referee's book?

Just drop the ball two or three yards *inside* the field of play as you retreat back to your position. By the time the opponent steps onto the field, picks up the ball, then steps back off the field, you and everyone else on your team should be properly positioned. The five seconds it takes the opponent to retrieve the ball takes all the danger out of a potential quick restart.

Is this a little thing?

Yes.

Do the little things matter?

Only when it comes to winning.

Note for Coaches: I'm dumbfounded by the amount of players who voluntarily hand the ball to the opponent in this situation. This should take you all of 30 seconds to explain and demonstrate to your team, and more importantly, it will save you countless migraines.

19

SOMETHING IS BETTER THAN NOTHING

You've exploded down the left wing and find yourself deep in the opponent's end with the ball at your feet and a half-step on the defender who is chasing you. The ball is perfectly positioned for you to stride into a cross. Your teammates are crashing into the box, clamoring to get onto the end of your serve. But at the critical moment you remember that you're not left-footed so instead of crossing the ball, you decide to cut it back onto your right foot. And that's where the play dies.

Usually the aforementioned attack dies because you cut the ball back between your body and the opponent's and the ball was tackled away. Sometimes the cutback works well enough to briefly shake the defender, but the ball gets caught underneath you and you end up trying to hit an unbalanced serve which never makes it into the danger area; or, you're forced to take another prep touch to get the ball out from underneath you and by the time you do hit the ball, the opposing team has gotten numbers back into the box and all of your teammates' runs have gone stagnant. Any which way you slice it, there's no happy ending.

So how do we fix it? Well, the easiest way to cure this problem is for you to learn to use your weak foot. Trust me; it really is as easy as it sounds. It just takes some practice. And even if your left foot will never be as good as your right, that's no reason that it shouldn't at least be functional. The day of the one-footed player has passed. If you're serious enough about soccer to read this book, then you need to be able to kick a ball with either foot. As I write this book, there's not a player on our Georgia team who can't smack a ball with either foot, and that includes the goalkeepers. These days, to be a good college soccer player, you need to be able to at least kick a ball with your weak foot.

Okay, so you're going to work on developing your weak foot but it may take a week or two before you see a noticeable improvement. So what are you going to do tomorrow when you're on the left wing and the situation begs for a cross?

You're going to cross the ball with your left foot.

Why?

Because something is better than nothing and nothing is what you'll likely end up with when you try to cut the ball back onto your right foot. When I'm out recruiting, I constantly see players make this mistake. Instead of taking the chance to put the ball into a dangerous area at a dangerous time, they fight to get the ball back onto their strong foot and come away with nothing. *Nothing!* You've got to cross the ball and give yourself a chance to get lucky.

If you cross the ball at the right time, you may not need to hit the perfect ball. Just putting the ball into a dangerous area may be enough to create some attacking havoc. At any rate, it's a heckuva lot better than getting absolutely nothing out of it.

Note for Coaches: We've all had players who refuse to cross the ball with their weak foot. Push-ups are a fantastic cure for this ailment when it happens during practice. The bench will work wonders if it happens during a game.

2 0

NOBODY'S HOME

Crosses can create wonderful scoring opportunities, and there is something ever so pleasing about hitting a beautiful cross over some defenders and just beyond the range of the goalkeeper. Crossing is a valuable skill and if you have it, well, good for you!

But try to remember that even the prettiest cross will do no good if you don't have a teammate getting into the box. Sometimes a forward will end up in a situation where she is out on the wing, close to the end-line, and a long way ahead of her pack of teammates. Too often that player doesn't evaluate what's actually happening inside the box and blindly smacks a cross; or she realizes that she has no help in the box but is so enamored of her own crossing ability that she crosses the ball anyway. Either way, the result is an epic fail.

If you find yourself in this situation, you've got to show some restraint and think about the big picture. As pretty as that ball might be sitting for you and as spectacular as your cross would most certainly be, it won't do your team any good if no one can get on the end of it. Are you with me on this? If you don't have any teammates bombing into the box, any cross you hit will likely be a donation to the opponent and your promising attack will have died a quiet, unspectacular death.

So what do you do?

Well, you put on the brakes and make the smart decision to accept reality. You think, *Well, crossing it to create a goal-scoring chance would have been the best thing, but since that's just not realistic, I'm going to keep the ball for my team and wait for some teammates to catch up to me so we can try to create a different type of goal-scoring opportunity.* So perhaps you circle back toward the sideline, pick your head up and find a teammate who is supporting you.

Yeah, it's not as glorious as the magnificent cross onto the head of a charging teammate, but it's a far cry better than gifting the ball back to the other team, right?

We discussed this earlier and it certainly applies here: When Plan A is no longer a useful option, just move along to Plan B.

Since we're on the topic, you may have a teammate rushing to get into the box but who is right on the borderline of not arriving there on time. In moments like this you may want to float your cross in a little higher than normal. The hang-time you put on the ball may give your teammate the chance to run underneath it.

Note for Coaches: When you do crossing sessions, demand that the crossers take a look before they serve. Way too many players hit blind crosses. Regardless of whether or not a teammate is in the box, one of the most important things a player can do before she hits that cross is to take a quick peek at what's happening in front of the goal. That quick look will provide her with valuable information as to where and when she should target her cross. It will also save her from crossing to an empty box.

21

SWIM UPSTREAM

We're going to continue with our crossing theme. Again we'll start with a ball that has gone out wide toward the corner and the prospect of a cross looks promising. In the interest of making this easier to understand, let's say you're coming straight up the middle of the field with the intention of eventually getting in front of the goal.

I want you to imagine that the soccer field is a flat table, and all of the players are marbles. Wherever the ball goes, the table tilts toward that side, so naturally, the marbles roll in that direction. This is never more true than in a potential crossing situation. Teammates move to that side to support the player on the ball; opponents move that way to either chase them or pressure the ball. Even the goalkeeper slides in that direction. If you were to look at it from above, the players would look like a school of fish swimming downstream.

At this point it would behoove you to know that as this crossing situation develops, the defenders are coached to see two things: you and the ball. This is an easy task for them when you and everyone else are moving toward the ball. All a defender has to do is follow you and she'll be able to see you and the ball in the same field of vision.

However, and this is the important part, if you run away from the ball (like the attacking midfielder in the diagram), now you give the defender one heckuva dilemma: if she turns to chase you, she can't see the ball; if she doesn't look away from the ball, she can't see you.

What the defender *should do* is turn away from the ball to stay tight to you. How often does she do that? Almost never.

At the moment when that critical decision needs to be made, very few defenders have the discipline to turn their back to the ball. As the current is pulling everyone in one direction, the defender is likely to drift right along with them, or at best, just freeze. It doesn't matter because either way, she's not going to keep up with you. If you can manage not to cave into the peer pressure of following all of the other little fishes, you're going to find yourself with a lot of free headers from crosses.

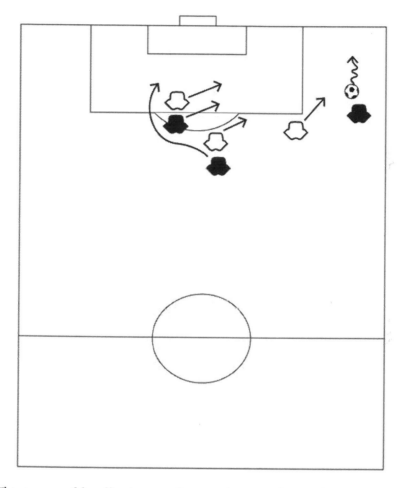

This is a terribly effective run for a trailing attacker such as a center mid, because by the time she's about to enter the 18, most of the other fishes are going to be paired off and swimming toward the ball. If you recognize this and swim upstream away from the ball, most of the defenders will just run right past you as if you were invisible.

Note for Coaches: I have found that getting this one to stick can be a lot harder than it sounds, and a lot harder than it should be. Players are just so programmed to get sucked into the ball's gravitational pull that convincing them to go the other direction can be very difficult. Running away from the ball is counterintuitive to them. On the upside, if you can convert just one of your players into believing that this run will pay dividends, it won't take long for her to see the reward. I've coached two players who basically made a living off this run. Once they realized how effective it was, there was no talking them out of it.

22

CAT AND MOUSE

If you're an attacking player, this bit of advice can change your life, so pay attention.

Let's say the ball is played out wide and a crossing scenario is developing, so you're about to go bombing into the 18 with visions of glory dancing in your head. A defender is goal-side of you and she is intent on not letting you get on the end of that cross.

Let's first look at this from the defensive point of view. When a crossing situation is developing, the defender certainly needs to stay goal-side. So usually there is a cushion of a few yards between you and her. But at a certain point, the defender should begin slowing down and allowing you to catch up to her. If the defender is doing her job well, the cushion between she and you will evaporate as you near the penalty spot. Ideally, from the defender's point of view, when the cross arrives, she should be shoulder-to-shoulder with you.

Let me tell you the mistake that most defenders make in this situation. Instead of focusing on being shoulder to shoulder with you when the ball arrives, your defender will focus on not letting you get between her and the goal. In effect, she turns this battle into a footrace to the goal. And when I say she 'turns' it into a footrace, I mean that often times she will literally turn her back to you and run toward her goal.

Now, would you like to know the mistake that you usually make? When she turns and runs to the goal, you usually go chasing right after her! Seriously! It looks like that defender ran off with your iPhone and you're trying to catch up with her!

Listen to me; that defender's job is to be tight to you when the ball arrives. If she wants to run away from you, let her! Just put on the brakes and let her run away from you and let the cushion between you and her grow bigger and bigger.

Let me ask you this: If you were playing a game of tag and you didn't want to be tagged, would you go chasing the kid who was *it*? Of course you wouldn't! That would be totally insane, right? Well, when you chase that defender, that's exactly what you're doing! Her job is to *tag* you; don't make that job any easier for her! The mouse doesn't chase the cat, right?

If that defender wants to run a race to the goal-line, *let her*! Blow her a kiss and wish her well. The further she runs away from you, the more she expands the landing zone for the cross and the more room you have to work with when you're on the end of it. All you have to do is stop running and a moment later you'll find yourself wide open.

Note for Coaches: Learning how to escape defenders in crossing situations is a critical skill for forwards because space inside the box is at a premium. Attackers have to appreciate that the difference between scoring and not scoring is often a matter of inches. Often times a forward can bait the defender into running that race to the goal by just shifting into a higher gear for a step or two.

23

THE GOALKEEPER'S BALL?

We were playing a spring friendly when one of the opponent's defenders, standing just in front of her own 18, launched a booming clearance that landed behind our line of defenders. Our center back was chasing the ball back toward our own goal with an opposing forward in hot pursuit. At the same time, our goalkeeper was charging out of our 18, intending to clear the ball. There came a moment when our defender had the chance to sweep the ball to the side and eliminate the threat, but our goalkeeper screamed, *"KEEPER!,"* so the defender deferred. Well, our keeper was a little bit late to the ball and ended up kicking it directly off the forward and it promptly ricocheted into our goal from 30 yards. It was a demoralizing way to give up a goal because it was entirely our own doing.

The next day I met with all of our defenders and issued a new policy: If the goalkeeper tells you it's your ball, it's definitely your ball. And if the goalkeeper says it's her ball, *it may still be YOUR ball!*

As a defender, you are judged first and foremost by how many goals your team concedes. If you have the chance to eliminate a threat, do it. Don't worry about whether or not your goalkeeper will be upset that you didn't listen to her because that doesn't matter. Don't take a situation that you know you can control and leave it up to someone else. If you can solve the problem, solve it. Being polite is not a good enough reason to give away goals.

You will also run into this conundrum with balls served into your 18. You'll be perched underneath the serve, ready to head it away, and then the goalkeeper will scream, *"KEEPER!,"* and then you have about half a second to make a decision. Look, if you know your goalkeeper will be there in time to comfortably handle the ball, then you may want to defer. But if there is even a thread of doubt in your mind and you know you can solve the problem, just do it yourself. You don't win games by being polite.

Note for Coaches: Players tend to deify goalkeepers and will often defer as soon as the goalkeeper opens her mouth. You've got to convince your defenders to solve their solvable problems. You can't donate great chances to the opponent and expect to win.

2 4

FIVE WILL SAVE YOU FIFTY

This is a situation that commonly happens to a winger or wide midfielder on the weak-side of the field when her team loses possession of the ball in its attacking half. To simplify things, let's just say that you are the right wing and your left wing has just conceded possession 30 yards from the opponent's goal.

As the opponent begins to get its attacking shape, you are likely going to be responsible for tracking/defending the left back. What you do will greatly influence what she does, so let me tell you how you can save yourself a whole lot of running.

When the transition occurs, that left back has to decide whether or not she wants to jump into the attack. Her decision is going to be largely influenced by the position you take up. If you quickly retreat to goal-side of her and give yourself a five-yard cushion, she'll probably lose interest in trying to run past you to join the attack. But if you fail to give yourself that head-start and she thinks she can get goal-side of you, believe me, she's gone! And once she goes, you've got to go with her.

Every time I'm out recruiting I see players make this mistake. Instead of immediately taking up a sound defensive position and deterring the opponent from making that run, the winger is slow to adjust and the outside back takes off like she was shot out of a cannon. Then the winger has to run fifty yards to catch up to her... and that's assuming she catches her before she's inflicted any damage!

Remember this: *Five will save you fifty!* An early five-yard sprint will save you the work of a fifty-yard sprint. If you do a little bit of work early, you'll save yourself the agony of doing a lot of work a moment later.

Here's the thing... you have to know that if you don't take up the proper position early, that opponent is going to be inspired to jump into the attack.

That's just how it is and how it's always been. But by positioning yourself goal-side and giving yourself a little bit of a cushion, that left back won't have any interest in trying to run by you because she knows she can't. You have a five-yard head start and that's just too much to overcome. Your sound positioning breaks her will to become an attacking presence.

Do the work early and save yourself the trouble of having to track the opponent fifty yards. Believe me, five will certainly save you fifty.

Note for Coaches: There's not a doubt in my mind that you have a player who makes this mistake. You need to convince her that a short burst of defensive transition is worth the effort and that her energy is better spent attacking than chasing.

25

BE FIRST TO YOUR CLEARANCES

Dear Forwards,

This is the really important part of your job that maybe no one has explained to you yet. And your failure to understand and execute this concept will exhaust your defenders and kill your team.

During any game there is going to be a time when the opponent sustains some type of attack in and around your goal area. It will be momentary madness. There will be crosses and shots and blocked shots and deflections and all types of pressure and chaos. And if your team is lucky, one of your defenders will have the chance to clear the ball up the field to relieve pressure. What happens next determines if the threat is eliminated or just recycled. It also determines a good bit of your value as a forward.

Too many forwards get lulled to sleep watching their defenders scramble to neutralize an attack. Then, when that magical clearance does come, they allow the opposing defender to step in front of them and the attack starts all over again.

The forward who is regularly first to her team's clearances is an absolutely priceless commodity! The ability to stay switched on — to *anticipate* that clearance and be the first player to it — and the ability to hold onto that ball for your team is a critical element in relieving pressure. If you're not good at this, you need to get good in a hurry.

It's easy to stay switched on when your team has the ball. But when your defense is under siege, you've got to remember what an important role you are about to play. Don't let your concentration lapse. You're not doing anyone any good by daydreaming about the goal you scored last week. When that ball pops back up the field, your team needs you to get to it and hold it.

Note for Coaches: The ability to be first to your team's clearances is the most underrated and under-coached tactical concept in soccer. Too many forwards don't understand just how important this part of their job is. When the ball is cleared, it's a chance to relieve the opponent's pressure and that's a really big deal. In any given game, if one team is really good at this and the other is really bad, the bad team is going to lose.

26

STEALING REST

Coaches love players who work their tails off! Of course we do! How could we not? Hopefully you are one of those magnificent grinders who can change the game simply on the strength of your work rate. If you are, your future is bright!

Now, what you have to keep in mind is that in terms of endurance, you are working on a finite tank of gas. If you drive too hard for too long, eventually you're going to run out of it. In the perfect soccer world you can run as hard in the last minute as you did in the first, and then have your tank go to 'E' precisely when the final whistle blows. That's in the perfect world. We won't always live there, but we sure can try.

As an educated soccer player, you need to look for opportunities to steal rest. The first part of that is not running foolishly. What do I mean by that? Well, when the ball you are chasing is 20 yards in front of you and destined to roll out of bounds, don't feel obliged to sprint after it. Sure, if you can get to it or come close to getting to it before it crosses the line, then have at it! But when it's no longer realistic, save your legs.

The same applies when your teammate kicks a ball that's going to roll into the opposing goalkeeper. There's no point in you sprinting from midfield to chase that ball when the goalkeeper is just going to pick it up before you arrive. Don't kill yourself running a fool's errand. It's one thing to die a hero. It's another matter entirely to die an idiot. (If your team is trailing, you may have to go running after the ball to force the goalkeeper to pick it up.)

When you are subbed out of the game, unless you are trailing on the scoreboard or there is some other urgent tactical matter at hand, don't feel obliged to sprint off the field like an Olympian. It's just a waste of energy. Try a casual jog instead.

Set pieces will afford you the opportunity to get a little bit of rest, but in those situations, particularly on defensive restarts, remember these words: *Get your position, then you rest.* Don't start resting until you take care of your positioning, otherwise you are going to get victimized by an opponent's quick restart.

Soccer doesn't give you very many opportunities to rest, so when those moments present themselves, take advantage of them. You need that tank of gas to get you through the whole game.

Note for Coaches: If a bunch of your players suffer from this malady, you have a good problem. We all love our workers, but teach them to sprinkle in a little bit of common sense.

27

ARE YOU TRYING TO KILL HER?

Your right wing has just sprinted 50 yards to jump into the attack. Then, because the attack broke down, she immediately had to turn around and sprint 60 yards back toward your goal where she slide-tackled the ball back for your team. The ball caroms directly to your feet and you see a wonderfully inviting opening, again up the right side. You pass the ball out there, 20 yards in front of that right winger, so she can run onto it and lead the next attack. So here's my question: *Are you trying to kill her?*

Okay, you're not actually going to kill her by playing that ball. Why not? Because she's not going to get to it. She probably won't even make much of an attempt to get to it. Why's that? Because she's exhausted! How do I know? Because she's standing there, hunched over, with her hands on her knees. She needs a break!

You've got to apply some common sense to the big picture. You've got to notice when a teammate has produced an intensive burst of hard work and then you've got to recognize that she could use a few seconds to catch her breath. In those moments of intellectual clarity, play the ball to one of your *other* teammates. As brilliant as your pass to the right side might have been, it's useless if your teammate can't run onto it.

Note for Coaches: This type of situation can occur in any number of the exercises you do at training, whether it's a full-field scrimmage or a possession drill. When you see it happen, stop the exercise and explain it to all of your players at once. This is one of those things you don't want to have to teach one player at a time. When a player has distinguished herself with a burst of exceptional effort, you reward her by letting her rest for a few seconds.

28

WHEN TO EXPEND SOME ENERGY

You can't play soccer at one pace. You constantly have to shift gears depending on the situation at hand. In Chapter 26 we discussed the times to save some of the fuel in your tank; now we're going to talk about an excellent time to burn some of it.

Let's begin with the simple soccer premise that the best time to win the ball is in the five seconds immediately after your team has lost it. Why? Because while you had the ball, the opponent was in its defensive shape, so its players were condensed into a smaller area. At the moment they won the ball, those players were still in that defensive shape. The idea here is to pressure the ball immediately, before the opponent has a chance to spread out and transition into an attacking shape. The sooner you can pressure the ball, the better chance you stand of winning it back and winning it back quickly.

Now let's take our premise one step further. The closer your team is to the opponent's goal when the ball is lost, the more condensed the opponent will be and the more time it will take them to transition into an attacking shape. Therefore, it only stands to reason that the closer you are to their goal when the ball is turned over, the more of an effort you and your teammates should make to put immediate pressure on the ball.

When the attack breaks down inside of the opponent's 18, we usually make two mistakes. First, we take a second to wallow in our misfortune before making the effort to pressure the ball. Then when we do pressure, we do it with something less than our very best effort. These are two very big mistakes.

Remember this: When you lose the ball in or near the opponent's 18, this is the time to expend some fierce energy and burn some fuel because your team has a golden chance to win the ball back right away!

Did you notice how I didn't say *"you"* have a golden chance? Nope, I said *"your team"* has a golden chance. And therein lies the rub. A lot of times a player won't put her full effort into pressuring that opponent unless she feels she can get there in time to tackle the ball. Stay with me on this one because this is a game-changer.

In this scenario, when the ball gets turned over and ends up on the foot of an opponent, her options are usually limited. The longer she has on the ball, the more viable her options become. With each passing fraction of a second, the chance of her success grows. The worst possible outcome for you is if that opponent, who has just won the ball, connects a clean pass or clearance.

When you provide immediate pressure, your objective isn't necessarily to tackle the ball from her. Your objective is to make sure that opponent doesn't connect cleanly to a teammate. The work you do to pressure isn't necessarily for you to win the ball, but it may very well be for one of your teammates behind you to win the ball. That's why you hit the gas and burn some fuel in this situation, even if you are certain that you won't get there in time to put in a tackle. Your very simple objective is to put that opponent under enough pressure that she hits a ball that is less than ideal. Yes, tackling the ball directly might be the best possible outcome, but if that doesn't happen, your work can still produce a valuable consolation prize: possession of the ball for your team deep in the opponent's end of the field. Teams that do an effective job of creating sustained pressure inside the penalty area produce a lot of goals.

When you find yourself in the situation described above, I want you to remember the ten-yard rule: if you are within ten yards of the ball, put the hammer down and go after it! Go after it with everything you've got! Burn some fuel and challenge that opponent to execute under maximum pressure, because a lot of times, she won't be able to do it. When you're that far down the field, don't worry about principles of defending or team shape; just go psycho and chase the ball. This isn't the time to worry about advanced tactics; this is the time to buzz around like the Tasmanian Devil and cause widespread panic. You might tackle the ball. You might block a clearance. You might force an unbalanced clearance that the opponent never gets off the ground. All types of wonderful things can happen when you expend some energy at the right times.

This work I am asking you to do, it requires you to be *selfless*. I'm asking you to pressure with everything you've got, *even if you know that you won't get there in time to tackle the ball,* just because it might give one of your teammates a better chance to win the ball. And just to be clear on this, all I'm really asking you is for about three seconds of an all-out sprint. It might not seem worth it, but it is. Please trust me on this one. It is absolutely worth it!

Note for Coaches: A player can have absolutely no talent and still effectively pressure the ball. The key to selling this one is in the word 'selfless.' Convincing your players that the work they do is for the big-picture reward is the key to them buying into this philosophy. When the ball is in the opponent's 18, obviously your main objective is to score. When the immediate prospect of scoring vanishes, the next objective should be to keep the opponent from coming out cleanly. You can create a lot of second and third chance opportunities by picking off outlet passes.

29

SPRINT EARLY

Let's continue with our theme of pressure. Let me give you a scenario. Again you're a forward.

The opposing center back, from the middle of her own half, knocks a pass to her outside back and you move to pressure her. You trot along at an 85% pace in pursuit of the ball. The outside back preps the ball, and just as she's about to step into her delivery, you burst into a full sprint to try and prevent or disrupt that delivery. And just as you arrive, the ball has left her foot. Your burst has been for nothing.

You have got to pick your times to expend your energy, and not every time is a good time to sprint to pressure. I understand that. What you need to understand is that if you almost got there on a trot, you probably would have gotten there on a sprint.

In these situations, the time to sprint isn't when the opponent has already received the ball; the time to sprint is when the ball is in transit!

Will you get there in time to win the ball? Sometimes. Not always. But the way I look at it, as the ball arrived at her feet, that outside back had several options ranging from best option to second-best option to third best and so on. If my work rate can take away her very best option, I've accomplished something. If it takes away her top two options, I've accomplished even more. Of course the best possible outcome for me is to force her into turning the ball over, which is why you should remember this:

It is much more nerve-wracking to receive a ball under pressure than it is to play a ball that has already been prepped. Whenever prudent, your objective should be to challenge that opponent into making a clean first touch with pressure bearing down on her. Challenge her technical ability. Challenge her to execute under duress. Get her focusing on the ball she's about to receive instead of where she can effectively play that ball. It can be very unsettling to think about controlling a ball when a freight train is bearing down on you. If she's not up to the challenge, often times you can pounce on her less-than-perfect first touch.

Now, you can help your own cause by recognizing some visual cues, and I'm going to give you a great one: *The more difficult the ball she is about to receive, the more likely her first touch will be bad.* If the ball she is about to receive is going to skip into her with a lot of pace, there's a pretty good chance that she'll have trouble executing a clean first touch. The same applies if the field condition is particularly bumpy, or if the ball is in the air with a lot of bend on it. As soon as you recognize that the ball presents a high degree of difficulty, instantly shift into high gear and look for a chance to pounce on a bad first touch.

And incidentally, if her first touch isn't good, don't let her off the hook. This is not the time to be patient in defending; this is the time to sell out and go after the ball. If she can't control the ball with her first touch, we don't want to give her a second chance.

Note for Coaches: This falls in line with the previous chapter. Players need to recognize when it's a good time to expend some of their energy. These calculated gambles can pay huge dividends. Nothing is more frustrating than seeing an opposing player get away with a bad first touch because we didn't recognize a good time to gamble away some of our energy.

3 0

WHEN ONE GOES, WE ALL GO!

In the last chapter we discussed the role of the person who can pressure the ball. Now let's assume that you are one of her teammates.

Let me say that from a player's point of view, there is nothing more frustrating than working your tail off to put an opposing player under pressure, only to have that opponent play past you to one of her teammates who is completely unpressured. That's just plain agonizing!

Remember when I said that you need to be selfless in your efforts to pressure the ball? Well, it's a lot easier to be selfless when you can count on the teammates who are behind you to position themselves to take advantage of your hard work. When you can't count on them to do that, putting in the work to pressure is a lot less satisfying. Quite frankly, it stinks!

When you see a teammate working hard to pressure the ball, you need to be working just as hard to capitalize on the less-than-perfect pass she is about to create. In these situations, all you need to remember is that *when one goes, we all go!*

When your teammate is working hard to press, join her! Join her by closing ground on the opponents who are in a position to receive the next pass. Don't give them a free-out by spectating. Don't just stand there admiring how hard your teammate is working! Anticipate the next pass and get involved! If you are one measly step late, the opponent will have the chance to break pressure and then all of your teammate's hard work will have been for naught. And that will make her sad.

Your teammates will only put in that extra effort to pressure for so long. If they aren't rewarded for their selfless effort, they're soon going to stop being so selfless and your team will suffer because of it. Don't just watch your friend working her butt off; join the fight! Pressure is a team thing, not an individual one.

Note for Coaches: One of my favorite games to train pressing high up the field is 10 v 10 possession, from 18 to 18, using the full width of the field. We put both teams into a system, such as a 4-3-3 or a 4-4-2. Every one-touch pass you connect in the opponent's half of the field is worth one point. This scoring system gives the players a strong incentive to keep the ball in the opponent's half of the field, and that requires players to quickly pressure the ball once possession is lost. It demands a concerted effort from every player, not just the player who is pressuring the ball.

31

REWARD YOUR TEAMMATE

Before you read the story I'm about to share, I want you to know that never once in the history of my soccer life did anyone ever refer to me as lazy. I was a grinder each and every step of the way. It is with a clear conscience that I say I worked my tail off! Are we clear on that? Good. Now you may read on.

I had a college teammate who was absolutely amazing on the ball. I'm not joking; this guy was truly fantastic. I genuinely loved watching him play. He could do things with the ball that no one else could. The problem was that he probably got that way because he hardly ever passed. We used to joke that when we had a game, there needed to be two balls on the field: one for this guy and one for everybody else. As talented as he was, sometimes it was very frustrating to be his teammate.

There was one game where he was trying to dribble his way around and through a couple of opponents at midfield. As he was engaged in this duel, I was working my tail off, sprinting back and forth to give him a passing option. Each time I would get into a good seam and ask for the ball, he would look at me and then decide to keep trying his luck as a solo artist. Three times I got myself into a position where he could have easily played me the ball to get out of this jam. Three times he decided not to pass me the ball. *Three times!*

I was five yards directly behind him when he finally lost the ball. As this was the latest in a long line of similar incidents involving the two of us, I was fed up. So as the opponent emerged from the scrum dribbling straight at me, I nonchalantly stepped aside like a matador dodging a bull and pointed him toward our goal.

A look of horrified disbelief came over my teammate's face. He couldn't believe that I had actually gotten out of the way of the opponent. I replied with a look of my own that said, *'Sorry, but I did my job. That's your problem, not mine.'* So my teammate went chasing after the guy.

I had worked extremely hard to help my teammate solve his problem. He chose not to reward my work and I wanted him to know that I wasn't happy about it. Was it a pretty bratty move? Oh, absolutely! Why did I do it? Because I'm human, and humans want to be rewarded for their efforts. We're funny like that.

When I was a college freshman, I had the ball in the middle third and one of my teammates made a 40-yard overlapping run to support me. I promptly ignored him and passed the ball to someone else. My coach told me that if I expected my overlapping teammate to keep working that hard for me, I'd better reward him with the ball. I felt my coach was making an excellent point.

Your teammates are human beings and they are going to act accordingly. They are more likely to repeat the behaviors for which they are rewarded, and less likely to repeat behaviors that reap no rewards, particularly if those behaviors require hard work. Understand that everyone's favorite part of playing soccer is touching the ball. When a teammate works hard for you, show her that you appreciate her efforts by giving her the ball. That's all the encouragement she'll need to continue working hard for you. On the other hand, if you continually go without rewarding her, she's going to stop doing all that hard work.

Note for Coaches: When it comes to long, unrewarded runs, outside backs are the most common victims of insensitive teammates. If you have an outside back who loves bombing forward (while not neglecting the part about sprinting back afterward to defend), you have a priceless commodity. Make sure her teammates periodically reward her hard work. All she really wants is a chance to touch the ball.

3 2

WHY OLYMPIC SPRINTERS DON'T DRIBBLE A SOCCER BALL

Here's the situation: The ball is in your team's defensive third. You're the center forward (although this applies to any position) and you're pressed up against the opponent's back line along the midfield stripe. Your right back hits a big clearance and the ball suddenly comes to your feet and your first touch can get you in behind the central defenders and put you in on a breakaway. So, how long should that touch be?

I sincerely hope that somewhere along the line you had a coach who explained to you that when you run, you are faster without a soccer ball than you are with a soccer ball. This is why Usain Bolt doesn't dribble a soccer ball when he is breaking world records. If he tried to run the 50-meter dash with a soccer ball at his feet, his times would be much, much slower, and believe me, he wouldn't be finishing at the front of the pack. Follow me so far? *You are faster without the ball!*

When you have a chance to run with the ball in the open field, you want to go as fast as you possibly can. Every time you have to adjust your running stride to push the ball ahead of you, you slow down. So your objective is to take as few touches as possible by taking the longest possible touches that will still allow you to keep control of the ball. Therefore, whenever possible, a ten-yard touch is better than a five-yard touch, and a fifteen-yard touch is better than a ten-yard touch. The fewer times you have to touch the ball, the faster you will go. Still with me?

Let's go back to the situation described at the top of this page and assume that your first touch was ten yards, long enough to put you behind the defenders. Now you're in a race to the goal, but you're at a distinct disadvantage, because the defender gets to run at her top speed. Why? Because she doesn't have to dribble a ball. But you do. So how do you negate her advantage? By taking as few touches as possible. And one 20-yard touch is better - *and faster* - than two ten-yard touches.

When I'm out recruiting, I see this all the time. An attacker has a chance to put herself in behind the entire defense with one long touch but instead decides to touch the ball with every third step, and that gives the defenders an opportunity to recover and get goal-side. Don't fall so in love with the ball that you're afraid to let it get more than a yard away from you. When there is room in front of you, don't be shy. Attack that space with some big touches to keep you at top speed. The bigger the better!

There's a time to dance with the ball, and then there's a time to just knock it out in front of you and go. When you confuse these moments, you waste time and, more importantly, opportunities.

Note for Coaches: To get this point across, have your fastest player race one of your slower players over thirty yards, but require the faster player to dribble a ball and touch it at least five times. Do this in front of the whole team. Just make sure your slower player isn't so slow that she can't win this race. Also, make sure your players know how to dribble at speed with the outside of their foot. This surface is the most conducive to keeping them in their natural running stride. A player who tries to dribble at speed with the inside of her foot isn't going to break away from anyone.

33

WHEN TO TACKLE EARLY

Many coaches teach their players to be patient in defending. We teach them to delay the attacker, funnel her to one side, make her predictable and wait for help. We remind them not to over-commit. This is all good advice — *most* of the time. Now, let me give you one excellent exception.

Sometimes you're going to be matched up with an opponent who has devastating speed and she knows how to use it. When you know you can't win a footrace against her, *don't let her turn it into a footrace.* When an opponent clearly outmatches you for pace, don't let her build up a head of steam. If you are close enough to tackle, *tackle early.* Tackle before she gets her balance and her bearings and has the chance to size you up and start running. Why? Because you might not get another chance! If you won't be able to catch her ten yards down the field, you may as well take your shot early.

You shouldn't just drift through soccer games oblivious to your surroundings. As the game progresses, you should be learning about your opponent and cataloging her strengths and weaknesses; figuring out ways to put yourself in the best possible position to win your individual battles against her. In a situation like the one described above, tackling early is a calculated risk that you might have to take. If you decide to tackle early, commit to it and go in with everything you've got!

Note for Coaches: This is one of those tactical situations that you'll probably notice before your player does. Just remind her that when she goes for that early tackle, she has to go in hard and fast to blow up that play. If she's going to gamble, she's got to go all in.

34

ONE MORE FOR THE GOALKEEPERS

Dear Goalkeepers,

Your one and only job is to give your team a chance to win the game. You do that by stopping shots and grabbing crosses and that sort of thing. You are first and foremost responsible for protecting your goal. Don't ever forget that. And don't ever voluntarily give the opponent a chance to threaten your goal!

Of course you already knew that. So why am I writing this chapter?

Somewhere along the line you decided that to be an effective punter of the ball, you needed to get your plant foot as close to the 18-yard line as humanly possible. And because neither you nor the officials are perfect, once every blue moon a goalkeeper is whistled for stepping outside of her box on a punt. And the only question is *WHY???*

Stepping beyond the 18 is an inexcusable error. So don't make it. And don't give the official the chance to even think you made it. Don't give him any reason to suspect that you've crossed that line, because let's face it, referees are not perfect. The question you have to ask yourself is, *"What's it really worth?"*

Let's say that you are right smack on the 18 when you punt the ball. When the ball leaves your foot, it's going to reach the midfield stripe. But if you release the ball 12 inches short of the 18, it's going to land 12 inches short of the midfield stripe. Not much of a difference, right? So why risk it? Why give the official any type of excuse to make a bad call? Are those extra 12 inches worth the opponent's free kick at the top of your box (not to mention the automatic yellow card that accompanies your foul)? Of course not!

Let me put it another way. Let's say you happen to be called for stepping beyond the 18 and someone happened to be videotaping the game. Wouldn't you feel much better if the video indisputably got you off the hook with your coaches and teammates?

In the first edition of *Soccer iQ*, I mentioned that goalkeepers should not hold the ball for more than six seconds when protecting a lead, just in case an official decides to whistle a delay of game penalty and award the opposing team a free kick from a very dangerous spot. How often is this foul called? Almost never. Almost. But *not* never. A few weeks after the launch of that book in the summer of 2012, the U.S. women were trailing Canada in the Olympic semifinal. With a 2-1 lead in the final ten minutes, the Canadian goalkeeper was whistled for that very infraction. The ensuing free kick resulted in a penalty kick against the Canadians. The U.S. tied the game and then went on to win in overtime. And the world was outraged! Well, at least Canada was.

This is the same thing! Stepping outside the box is almost never called, but it's not *never* called. So why risk it? Why risk putting your team in that situation? Take twelve inches off your punt. What's the big deal?

Note for Coaches: When that call was made against Canada, do you remember how everyone was saying that they've never seen a goalkeeper whistled for that type of time wasting? Well, in the spring of 2011, our team at UGA had a friendly against the Atlanta Beat of the WPS. In the latter part of the second half, the Beat goalkeeper was whistled for that same infringement. So yes, it does happen. More importantly, three of the players in that friendly were also involved in that controversial 2012 Olympic match; two Americans, and one Canadian. My point is this: *U-S-A!!!*

THE IMPOSSIBLE PASS - PART 2

In Volume 1, I tried to dissuade you from asking for the Impossible Pass. Now I'm going to try to dissuade you from attempting to play the Impossible Pass.

In the diagram, the center forward has received the ball at midfield and is facing her own goal with a defender on her back. Instead of supporting underneath her, the right wing goes flying by her, screaming for the ball. At this point the center forward has three basic options:

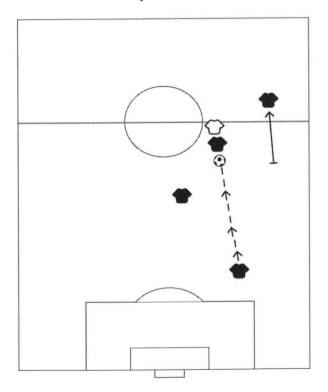

1. Hold the ball and figure her way out of the pressure.
2. Lay it off to a teammate (other than the right wing) who is providing support underneath.
3. Try to spin and play a ridiculously difficult ball into the right winger.

If a majority of players would choose options 1 or 2, I wouldn't be writing this chapter. However, most players are convinced that they can successfully connect this pass and therefore habitually give the ball to the other team. Has your coach ever told you to play the way you face? Yeah? Well, this is why.

There are two really big problems with playing this ball, and the first problem is so big that you rarely make it to the second one. The reason that this pass almost never works is because it's so stinking predictable! It's just way too easy for the defender who is on your back to read your body language when you are facing one direction and trying to play the ball in the opposite direction. That defender has a great view of everything. She saw the right wing go flying by and knows that you'd like to pass her the ball. Then she sees you trying to contort your body to get around the ball and she knows what's coming. Then all she has to do is take one step to the side and she's totally eradicated your passing lane. It is the easiest pass in the world to defend which is a really good reason for you to stop attempting it.

The second problem is that you are playing a blind pass. One great reason to play the way you face is that you can see all of the pieces of the puzzle. When you are facing south and trying to play north, that's no longer the case. So, if you miraculously get the ball past the first defender, there is often a second defender waiting to accept your gift and you had no idea that she was even there.

Somewhere along the line you have probably played this pass and it's actually been successful, so let me remind you of one of the tenets of soccer: Just because you got away with it, that doesn't make it right. This pass is a low, low, LOW percentage pass. It almost never works. That means it's almost... IMPOSSIBLE. If you play this pass and it works, it's not because you made a smart play. It's because you got lucky.

Note for Coaches: If you read *Volume 1*, you'll recall a chapter called Better Than Square that focused on providing easy passing angles underneath the target who is receiving the ball. If that support isn't there, the target is more prone to attempting this absurd pass. You've got to talk her out of it because it just won't work.

3 6

THE TOO-SHALLOW CROSS

This is one attacking mistake that you'll quickly regret making, so pay attention.

When you have the ball deep down the flank and a crossing situation is presenting itself, you'll ideally have three potential targets inside the 18. You'll have someone arriving at the near post, someone floating in at the far post, and then a trailing runner arriving at the penalty spot. Hopefully their positioning will look something like this diagram.

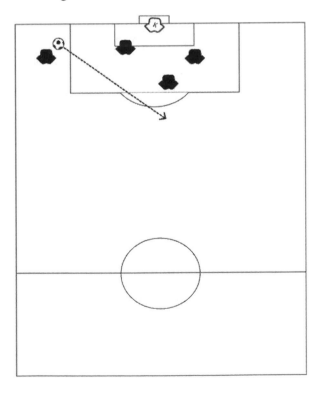

Obviously you hope to connect your cross with one of those three targets because this can be a fantastic attacking opportunity. But even as you are in the throes of a magnificent attack, you've still got to consider a big-picture ramification. You see, if your serve comes in behind the near post runner, there's no great tragedy in that. And if it comes in behind the far post runner, it's not going to kill you. But if you hook that serve to the point that it arrives behind the trailing runner (as indicated in the diagram), well, now there's an excellent chance that your team has some real problems.

Look, I know you weren't trying to hit a horrible cross, but this is one of those moments when you have to leave yourself a little margin for error because you are smart enough to think about the big picture. The too-shallow cross is one of the great undocumented calamities of soccer and you'll be a smarter player once you understand it.

Let me begin by sharing my unofficial premise that whenever someone hits a too-shallow cross, the ball always ends up in the opponent's possession. I don't know why that is, but I've seen it enough times to believe in its indisputable truth. It's probably a type of cosmic punishment sent down from the soccer gods for hitting such a bad serve. Regardless, let's begin by saying that when you hook your cross behind that trailing runner, the other team gets the ball in the central corridor of the field. That's the first problem, and the fun is just beginning.

Remember in Chapter 1 when we discussed the importance of numbers? Well, this one is all about the numbers. The most dangerous counterattacks materialize when the attacking team has big numbers committed forward. The too-shallow cross will often lead to a frenzied counterattack for precisely that reason. When the cross ends up behind the trailing runner, it immediately subtracts four attacking players from the equation. You crossed the ball which means you are standing out by the corner flag, so you're in no position to do much defending. As for your three teammates, well, they were all running one direction when your cross sailed behind them, so they aren't going to do much good either. So immediately your team is minus four, and oh, incidentally, you only have seven teammates left to deal with the situation. Then, every one of the opposing defenders who jumps into the counterattack before you or your teammates can recover adds a plus-one to the opponent's side of the equation. If just one of those defenders can hop up into the attack, you've just created a five-person swing for the opponent. Believe me, that's a massive swing... and a potential disaster for your team... and you did it all with one swing of your foot. Pretty impressive.

Okay, that's a close as I ever want to come to writing a math book, so I hope you stuck it out. The point is that you have to make sure your cross comes in somewhere between the trailing runner and the goal. If you hook it behind that trailing runner, your team has big problems.

Note for Coaches: I don't see this very often at the college level, but I've seen it enough to know that I don't like it one bit. The percentage of too-shallow crosses that generate dangerous counterattacks is uncanny. Every one of them looks like a big, fat jailbreak. Your crosser has to put the ball in front of that trailing runner if for no other reason than it gives that player a chance to defend if the attack breaks down.

3 7

POP THE BALL

Want to distinguish yourself in the world of female soccer players? Want to separate yourself from the herd? Want college coaches to see you in their dreams? It's easy. When you tackle, try to pop the ball.

There are legions of technically gifted female soccer players that dribble well and shoot for power and pass with accuracy. As a college coach who spends a good bit of time recruiting, my problem is that 99% of them are soft. They don't tackle with courage or conviction. If they tackle at all, it's because they've been left with no other choice. They remind me of the person who is about to donate a pint of blood and endures the unpleasant prick of the needle because there is no way around it. She grits her teeth and hopes that it's over as quickly as possible. That's how too many of you tackle – like you just want to get it over with. That's what we refer to as a 'half-tackle.' And when you tackle like that, you run into two problems: One, you will most likely lose the challenge; and two, you're begging to be injured. When you wave a foot at the ball while the opponent goes in full bore, there's an excellent likelihood that your knee is going to pop about three different ligaments. You are way safer committing your entire body to the challenge and putting all of your weight behind it. I've seen way too many serious injuries from half-tackles.

Tackling is just as much a part of the game as dribbling, passing, shooting and heading. You shouldn't ignore it. And since you're going to have to do it somewhere along the line, you may as well do it right. When the time comes to tackle, set aside your fears and throw yourself into that tackle with everything you've got. Don't just tackle to win the ball; tackle to pop it!

Do yourself a favor and stop thinking of tackling as simply a way to get the ball back from the opponent and start thinking about it for what it can be: a total momentum changer. One thundering tackle can change a game. It can breathe life into your team. It can put the wind at your back and inspire your teammates and ignite the crowd. And if that's not reason enough for you to want to tackle, try this one: Coaches will love it!

We all love the players who are fearless into tackles. It's not just about the moment they win the ball; it's a statement about the type of competitors they are. Players who regularly choose courage are winners. They are the people we want on the field when the game is on the line because they aren't afraid to risk their physical well-being in the name of competition.

If you want to be different than all of those other girls looking for college scholarships, I assure you there is a large market for the female player who enjoys dropping the hammer, because they are both so valuable and oh so rare.

The ability to tackle with power and conviction will make you different. It will separate you from the endless legion of soft, technical players who look for any excuse to bail out of a 50-50 challenge. Not everyone in society can be an artist. Ditch-diggers do important jobs, too. The same goes for soccer. Want to make a name for yourself? Be a warrior. You'll quickly become a hot and valuable commodity.

Note for Coaches: If you have a player who blows up opponents on every 50-50 ball, please don't talk her out of it.

38

MIDDLE-THIRD FREE KICKS

This is one you'll have to discuss with your coach, but I'm just going to give you my opinion on free kicks from the middle-third.

More often than not, when a team is awarded a free kick just to their attacking side of midfield, a bunch of players jumble up around the 18 and then someone lumps a high, floated serve towards the scrum. Do these hopeful launches produce goals? Yes. Sometimes they do. Even against my own teams they have. But I hate them anyway. I'll tell you why.

In my entire soccer playing career, no coach ever said, "Now that you have clear possession of the ball, I want you to hoof it really far that way and see what happens." We play possession games all the time and at no point do we ask the players to occasionally just put the ball up for grabs. My point is this: I don't see the logic in taking a ball that is 100% ours and making it 50% theirs.

Are there exceptions? Absolutely. If your team has a couple of players who are great in the air, then sure, maybe you lob it up there and see what they can do with it. You can create flick-ons and second-ball opportunities. Some teams feast on these types of restarts and I would never try to talk them out of it, but those teams are few and far between. By that same token, if it's late in the game and you're desperate to find that tying goal, sure, it may be time to try the Hail Mary.

As for me, I think that when the referee whistles that free kick at midfield, you're better off putting the ball on the ground and quickly passing it to a teammate... just like you would do any other time you had 100% possession of the ball in that area of the field. If the opponent organizes itself quickly enough to take that option away from you, then you'll have a wonderful reason to launch that 50-50 ball into the box.

Note for Coaches: I'm perfectly prepared to accept your disagreement with this chapter. To each his own.

39

LATE RESTARTS

You're down a goal late in the game, but your attacking pressure has produced a corner kick with 30 seconds left on the clock. You quickly grab the ball and set it in the corner arc. In a blind panic you serve the ball as fast as you can because there are now only 25 seconds left. You did good, right?

Ummm... no.

Okay, let's figure out why.

What often happens in this situation is the player on the ball feels the pressure of the clock and wants to put the ball in front of the goal as quickly as possible, so she serves the ball when only three or four of her teammates have gotten into a decent position. Therefore her team is vastly outnumbered in the landing zone and the opponent ends up with an easy clearance.

When you get a late restart like a corner kick or a free kick, you want to make it count, particularly if you are trailing. It may be your last chance to put the ball in front of the opponent's goal, so you've got to give your team the best possible chance. To do that, you need your teammates to get in front of the goal, and to get there, they need time. They don't need a lot of time, but they probably need another ten seconds to get into the box and get themselves somewhat organized. On some teams, the most dominant headers are defenders. You certainly want to give your best headers a chance to get in front of the goal before you hit that serve.

Listen up... Once the ball is spotted to take that corner or that free kick, 30 seconds is an eternity. It's enough time to get all of your teammates into the box with another 15-20 seconds to spare. So don't panic. Don't waste your last chance to produce a goal. Just stay calm, take a deep breath, make sure you've got the right people in place, and then deliver your serve.

The objective is to take just enough time to make sure the right people are in place, and not one second more. The hope is that your team either scores directly or has enough time to produce a second chance opportunity if the ball drops into the area or if there's a rebound.

Will you score? Maybe. Maybe not. But you've got to give your team the best possible chance. Don't squander this opportunity by needlessly hurrying the kick.

Note for Coaches: We had this exact scenario come up a few years ago. Down by a goal, we rushed a corner kick with 30 seconds left and the ball went straight out of bounds. When we reviewed it on video, we made the players watch the final 25 seconds of nothingness ticking away so they could get an idea of how much time we actually had to work with. That got the point across pretty well.

40

WHO GOES IN THE WALL?

If the opponent is awarded a free kick in an area that warrants a wall, make sure you've got the right people in the wall. For the purposes of this chapter, let's just assume that all of the free kicks will be taken from within 25 yards of the end-line.

First of all, you need to determine if the restart is more likely to be a shot or a serve. I can't walk you through every possibility, and when it comes to walls, there are as many exceptions as there are rules, so let's just stick to some generalities. Typically, the more centrally the ball is spotted, the more likely that the opponent will shoot directly. The wider the ball is spotted, the more likely that you'll see a serve. Are you still with me?

Incidentally, you also need to pay attention to whether the referee has awarded a direct or indirect free kick. Indirect kicks are more likely to become serves.

If you think the opponent is going to shoot directly, you're probably going to want your tallest players in the wall. If you think that you're more likely to see a serve, then you want to make sure your best headers *aren't* standing in the wall.

Often times your tallest players are also your best headers, and that's where this can get tricky. The opponent isn't going to announce its intentions, so you've just got to make your best educated guess as quickly as possible so you can start getting organized.

Note for Coaches: It's my personal belief that having your best headers out of the wall is more important than having your tallest players in it. I can count on one hand the amount of times I've seen an opponent's direct kick hit one of my players in the head. If there is 50/50 shot or serve proposition, I want my best headers out of the wall and in front of the goal. Scoring directly from a free kick is pretty darn difficult, particularly if that kick isn't lined up centrally. I'd rather challenge the shooter to hit a great free kick and put my best headers where they can do the most good.

Incidentally, if the opponent puts two or more people on the ball, it's a good idea to have one player assigned to charge the ball if it is just tapped.

41

SETTING YOUR WALL

A lot of coaches prefer that the goalkeeper line up the wall for defensive restarts. I am not one of them. On the off-chance that your coach is like me, you need to know how to line up a wall.

Let me first say why I'm not a fan of the goalkeeper lining up the wall. For starters, I've seen about a half-dozen goals where the free kick was taken while the 'keeper was hugging the post and lining up the wall. Yeah, I know that a goalkeeper should make sure that the referee has told the attacking team to wait for a second whistle before she starts lining up a wall, but what *should* happen and what *does* happen can be two entirely different matters.

The other reason I don't like goalkeepers lining up the wall, and this is the only reason that you really need to know, is that way too often they just get it wrong. I've seen countless examples of goalkeeper-aligned walls that either leave room on the near post or are set so wide that three players are standing wide of the near post. Either way, it's no good. I'd rather have my goalkeeper focusing on the job of keeping the ball out of the net. So for this chapter, let's just do it my way and have you line up the wall.

There are two ways that field players mess this up: they either don't know where to line up the wall, or they know where to line it up but are bad at communicating their instructions. We're going to solve both of those problems right now. So here's the recipe for lining up the wall in six easy steps.

Step 1 – Know who your near post player will be. She's the only one you actually have to lineup. Everyone else will just squeeze up against her.

Step 2 – Stand about six or seven yards behind the ball, not goal-side of it, so you can see both the ball and the goal. Technically you're supposed to be ten yards from the ball in all directions, but most officials will let you steal a few yards as long as you're not interfering with the kick.

Step 3 — Start lining up your near post player. You don't need to be perfect right now. You're going to have to make adjustments once the referee sets the distance for the wall. Right now you're just trying to get the post player close to where she'll eventually be set.

Step 4 — You want to create an imaginary straight line that runs from your feet, through the ball and to the near post. Pay attention here, because this is the important part. *You want that line to run through your post player's inside shoulder.* Your job is to maneuver the near post player until her inside shoulder is on that line. This will put the frame of her body wide of the post, and that should be enough to protect against a bender into the near post.

Step 5 — Communicate clearly and concisely. Instead of waving your hand in front of your chest — because that's horribly confusing — act like a police officer directing rush hour traffic. Extend your arm out to the side and point in the direction that you want the post player to move. When you talk to her, use your most commanding voice. You only need to use two words: 'Step!' and 'Stop!' So if you want your post player to move to your right, point to your right and say, "Step! Step! Step! Stop!" If she overshoots the target spot, just point the opposite way and say, "Step," until you have her properly positioned. Once she is set, give her the thumbs-up and everyone else can stack up against her.

Step 6 — Wait! Wait until the referee is satisfied with the distance that your teammates are from the ball before you absolve yourself of your duty. If the referee pushes your wall back a single step, your post player will be misaligned and your wall will be off. Additionally, after the ball has been set, a sneaky attacker might pick up the ball to 'check it for air,' and then reset it in a different spot. If that happens, once again your wall will be off. Wait until all the dust settles before leaving your post, then go find someone to mark.

Remember, the imaginary line should run from your feet, through the ball, through post player's inside shoulder and into the near post. If you can get that right, you've set a good wall.

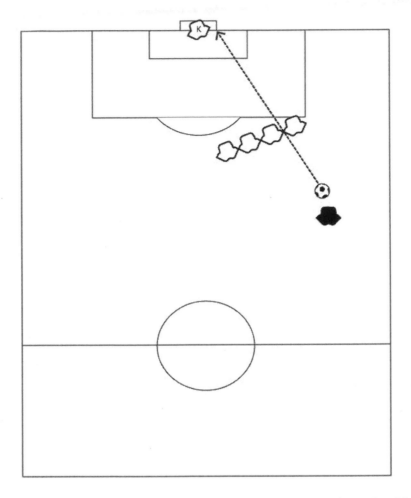

Note for Coaches: I consider this a basic life skill that every player should possess — like the ability to change a flat tire — just in case the need arises. Even if you prefer to have your goalkeeper set the wall, the next coach your players have may not, so think of this as a way to prepare your players for their soccer futures. The inability to quickly assemble a proper wall could lose you a game. It's worth taking five minutes of a practice to give everyone a turn at learning how to do this.

42

TIMING YOUR CHECKING RUN

In this chapter we are discussing a situation where an outside back has the ball and you, as the forward, will be checking back to her for the next pass. This is a fundamental concept that a lot of players – not just forwards - really struggle with, so let's figure it out.

As a forward, you need to be excellent at receiving balls when you have pressure on your back. Controlling the ball when it arrives at your feet while a defender is clawing at your back is a very advanced technical skill and one you'll need to develop. But I'm talking about what happens before the ball actually gets to you. I'm talking about the *timing* of your run back to the ball.

Let's start with the simple premise that receiving the ball 30 yards from your opponent's goal is better than receiving the ball 40 yards from your opponent's goal, and receiving it 40 yards from their goal is better than receiving it 50 yards from their goal. The closer you are to the opponent's goal when you receive the ball, the more likely your team is to score. Makes sense, yes?

Now your center back is passing a square ball to your right back, and you want the next pass to come to you, so you are going to check toward the right back. At the moment you begin checking, every step you take towards the ball is another step further away from the goal you are attacking. The trick is being able to check back hard and fast without killing too much ground between you and your teammate. If she can successfully play you a 30-yard pass, you don't want to ask for a 20-yard pass. Still with me?

So, BEFORE you start checking back, the question you need to ask yourself is this: *Is she ready to play me?* In other words, does she have control of the ball; is it prepped properly; is she balanced; and has she seen me? If the answer is no, hold your ground and stay away from her. There is no point in checking back to your teammate until she is prepared to play you the ball, because every step you take towards her puts you another step further away from the goal you are attacking. The trick is to check back hard while taking as few steps as possible back toward your own goal.

Too many forwards check back too soon, kill too much ground, and then realize that in half a second they will be running right on top of their teammate. Then, in an effort to correct their mistake and preserve some territory, they slow down or stop as the ball is en route. Because they slow down, the defender who was on their back is now stepping in front of them to intercept the pass. To keep defenders from stepping in front of you, you need to get the timing right.

Here's a good rule of thumb: *Start late and arrive fast.*

Don't check back until your teammate has prepped the ball. Be patient and hold your ground up high. Give her the time to get control of the ball and get balanced. This should only take her about a second and a half. While she's going through that process, take a few steps to check *away* from her. Put more distance between your teammate and the ball. That way, when you check back *at a sprint*, you receive the ball higher up the field than you would have otherwise.

Once your teammate has prepared the ball, check back to her hard and fast.

That's really all there is to it: Be patient. Hold your ground. Check away first, then when your teammate is ready to play you the ball, check back AT A SPRINT.

In the above example we were talking about a situation where the passer had to take at least two touches. However, if the situation dictates that the passer should or must play the ball with one touch, then by all means, check back earlier to shorten the distance of the pass. Regardless, you still need to sprint to get there.

Note for Coaches: This problem is a plague at nearly every level of soccer. In large part, the timing of the checking run dictates whether or not the movement is successful. Most players check back too early. Here is a simple drill to get your players started on properly timing their runs and holding the ball under pressure. It is an easy exercise to build on to so you can incorporate it into shooting, crossing and combination exercises.

The large grid is 30x10 yards that includes a 10x10 yard grid at one end. The defending player must stay goal-side of the target player until the ball is played forward. The two attacking players inter-pass a few one-touch, square balls until one of them decides to take a prep touch and then play into the target. The target's job is to hold her ground up high, and then time her checking run back to the ball. She must not leave her small grid when coming back to the ball, so she has to be strong and hold off the defender. When the entry pass is made, the second attacker runs up to support the attack. Once the second attacker arrives in the small grid, the two attackers play 2v1 and try to dribble the ball across the endline. If the defender wins the ball or the ball leaves the small grid, the play is dead. To further challenge the target player, make the big grid longer and shorten the small grid, or make the supporting attacker do a sit-up before starting her run.

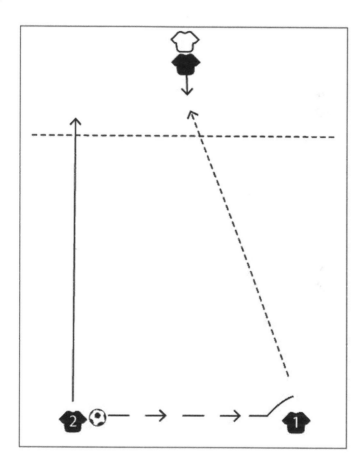

43

START OFFSIDE AND GET STEALTHY

In the last chapter we spoke about timing your checking run. Now we're going to discuss how to improve your starting position before you make that run.

Again, you're a forward and you're hovering somewhere near the midfield stripe as your teammates possess and advance the ball. Eventually they are going to look for an opening to play you the ball and you'll check back to receive that pass.

As we've already learned, the higher you can start up the field, the better. The higher you start up the field, the higher up the field you will be when you receive the ball. The higher up the field you receive the ball, the closer you are to the opponent's goal. So if your team has the ball 35 yards out in front of your own goal, wouldn't it make sense to start at the opponent's 18? Of course it would because you could really stretch out the opponent and give your teammates more time and space with which to play. Except there's one really big problem with that, right? That darned offside rule. Eventually the defense will stop retreating with you and you'll be wandering into an offside call. Okay, so in that particular situation we can't start all the way up at the opponent's 18, but there is certainly some wiggle room that we need to exploit.

The problem with starting from an onside position is that the defenders can always see you and the ball in the same picture. That makes everything very predictable for them. And *'predictable'* is just another word for *'easy.'*

Understand this: *Defenders hate it when they can't see you and the ball in the same picture.* That simple, solitary concept is the basis for this whole chapter. When they can't see you, they have to find you, and that means they have to look away from the ball, and they hate doing that most of all! And if you're not consistently doing things they hate, then you're not too good at your job.

When you are a forward, you are certainly allowed to start in an offside position. You just have to get back onside before a teammate passes you the ball. So, instead of floating in front of the line of defenders, float a yard or two behind them. Get stealthy. Move from side to side as if you're playing a game of peek-a-boo. Keep popping up in different spots. Then, when the time comes to check back to the ball, those defenders will never see you coming. By the time you reappear in the defender's field of vision, you'll be checking back at a full sprint and she'll be at a standstill. That means you'll probably get to take an unpressured first touch, and that's a very good thing.

Note for Coaches: Almost nobody does this, but if you think about it, it's actually a very simple concept. You just need a forward who reads the game well enough to know when that entry pass is about to be delivered and will check back at the right time. If you happen to find the forward who will commit to playing like this, it won't be long before she embraces the concept because all types of opportunities open up when you learn to hide from defenders.

44

STEMMING THE TIDE

Play soccer long enough and you develop the ability to sense swings in momentum. Let me give you a scenario that is applicable to this chapter.

You're being outplayed by the opponent. There are ten minutes left. The long and short of it is that they are the better team, but they aren't having their best day in front of goal and against the run of play, your team scores to take the lead. You celebrate with the goal-scorer and then take up your position in your half of the field as you await the tap-off. And as you come down from the euphoria of the goal, you are suddenly hit over the head with the reality that you may have just woken the sleeping giant. You can feel the new sense of urgency that has just registered with the opponent. You know that they are about to throw everything and the kitchen sink at you. For the next few minutes, your team is going to be hanging on for dear life.

Have you ever been a part of a moment like this? Chances are that you've been on both sides of this coin at some point or another, so you know what I'm talking about. Let me give you some advice: The very first chance you get, knock the ball as far down the field as you can, preferably wide of the 18 to keep it away from the goalkeeper. When the opponent is fueling up on desperation and it's time to make your stand, the last place you want that ball is in your end of the field. You've got to counter their enthusiasm by making them retreat. That high-octane, nervous energy that they are running on won't last forever. Make them burn a bit of it off by retreating into their own end to retrieve the ball.

An inordinate amount of goals are scored in the five minutes immediately following another goal. When the opponent is about to outmatch you emotionally, your first objective should be to survive that five-minute window. Instead of trying to match their emotional frenzy — because you won't — settle for taking the air out of their sails. Remember, they were better than you to begin with;

now they are angry and inspired to boot. This is not a great match-up for you. Let them deal with the frustration of one busted attack after another. Chip away at their spirit. It won't take long for them come down from that emotional high and then you'll be back to playing on somewhat level terms. Plus, you probably have some teammates who began experiencing a panic attack five seconds after you took the lead; this will give them a chance to calm down and resurrect their confidence.

Note for Coaches: I fully anticipate your backlash from this chapter, mainly because it sounds like I'm advocating that you abandon your style, and logic says that you shouldn't need to. Yeah, that's pretty much it in a nutshell. I wholeheartedly agree that logic says you shouldn't have to proceed this way. I also know that I wouldn't put all my eggs in the logic basket when it comes to soccer. Logic is hardly reliable when you factor in the human element. I confess that I don't have the science to back me up on this one, but I've been on both ends of this situation a whole bunch of times and experience has taught me that if you don't get the ball out of your end at the first possible opportunity, there's a reasonable chance that you'll be picking it out of your net soon thereafter. If you think this chapter is utter nonsense, don't sweat it. We can simply agree to disagree. Just rip out this page and proceed to the next chapter.

45

THE INEXCUSABLE OFFSIDE

Wingers, this one is especially for you, so if you want to drive your coach completely mental, ignore my advice.

When you are standing wide of the entire line of opposing defenders, please stay onside. When you can see all the defenders and the ball in the same field of vision (as in the diagram), there is absolutely no excuse for going offside. None! All you have to do is look across at the deepest defender and stay even with, or in front of her, until the ball has been played. That's it. I could teach my dog to do that, and my dog is kind of an idiot.

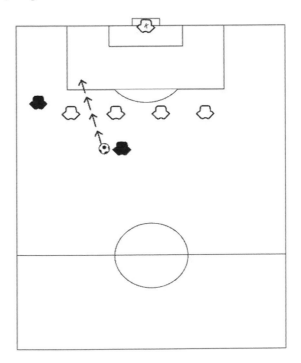

A lot of things have to go right to build a successful attack, and a lot of those things aren't completely under your control, but this one is. Don't self-destruct by being careless. Remember to take a look across that line of defenders. It's part of your job.

When your carelessness in this situation dismantles your team's attack, there's an excellent chance your coach will let you know about it.

Note for Coaches: Don't you hate when players do this? I wish I could give you some advice on this one, but if a player understands the offside law and still gets this one wrong, she's just being irresponsible.

46

THE BACKPEDALING DEFENDER

Throughout your soccer-playing career, you'll frequently hear coaches asking you to recognize 'visual cues.' Visual cues are brief moments that foretell the immediate future. They are 'if-then' moments that should signal you to do one thing or another. For example, if the opposing center midfielder takes a big prep touch and looks deep down the field, then there's an excellent chance that she's going to hit a long ball. That visual cue should signal the opponent's line of defenders to retreat. Stay with me because I'm about to give you one of the best visual cues in all of soccer, and my guess is that no one has ever mentioned it to you. This is the closest thing to a soccer 'secret' that I have to offer. Forwards, you should pay close attention to this one.

We'll continue on with our example from the previous paragraph and say that you are the center forward on the midfielder's team. Your midfielder plays that long, flighted ball down the field. The opposing center back is positioning herself to head it. What do you do?

Well, if the defender looks comfortably perched under the ball, you may want to put on the brakes and stop underneath her and play for the second ball. BUT... and this is a big one... if you notice that the defender is starting to backpedal, and she's starting to lean backwards as she backpedals, there's an excellent chance that she is going to either completely miss the ball or that she is going to inadvertently flick it on toward her own goal. Either way, that backpedaling, backward-leaning defender is your visual cue to get on your horse and run right past her, because there's an excellent chance that's where the ball is going to be.

It has been my observation that if the defender has to backpedal more than four steps, the ball is going to end up behind her. As an intelligent and opportunistic forward, you need to recognize this as an excellent time to gamble and sprint right past her. If you do, you'll not only create some stellar goal-scoring opportunities, you'll also look like a savant.

These moments happen on a fairly regular basis, but they are almost never capitalized upon because attackers just assume the defender will head the ball so they take up a position underneath her. More often than not, that's exactly how it goes. But if you catch that defender starting to backpedal and you notice the telltale lean, believe me, she's in trouble and you need to get running.

Want some bonus info? Well, it has also been my observation that a defender who misjudges one header in this fashion will likely misjudge more than one. If you miss out on your chance the first time, don't give up hope. Just be on the lookout for that defender to be in the same situation later in the game. And this time, when you see her backpedaling, make her pay for it!

Note for Coaches: This theory is also pretty reliable when it comes to goal-keepers fielding high crosses, particularly in a crowd. When the goalkeeper starts backpedaling, have an attacker positioned right behind her, waiting for the ball that slips through her hands.

47

LIVE TO PLAY ANOTHER DAY

Chances are you're at an age when you've already been involved in a game like this. Your team is winning by two goals, there are ten minutes left in the match and the other team is very frustrated by the way things are going and they are frustrated by the referee and their tempers are reaching critical mass. Then your team adds another goal and the opponent knows it can't win the match, so its players start turning their attention to chopping you in half.

The referee won't always do a very good job of protecting you. Sometimes he just can't. Either way, you've got to recognize when the other team has stopped caring about the result and started caring about hurting you. And the better you are as a player, the more likely you are to be a target. When the game has devolved into a kick-fest, you have got to recognize it and you've got to adapt. At that point it's time to move into survival mode.

I've seen some horrible injuries happen when a game is already out of reach. A player is losing and frustrated and she's mad at the ref and she's mad at the fans who are tormenting her, so she goes completely mental and tries to break someone's leg. And in soccer, more than most other sports, if your aim is to injure someone, it's pretty easy do.

You should be able to recognize when an opponent is about to go off the beam. And when that moment arrives, above all else, PROTECT YOURSELF!

But how?

I'm glad you asked.

First and foremost, don't hold onto the ball. When you dwell on the ball, you are inviting disaster and it's just not worth it. Play with one touch if at all possible. Don't let opponents get close enough to tackle you. Just get the ball away from you as quickly as you can. If you are a compulsive dribbler, this is an excellent time to highlight your selflessness as a passer of the ball. You've already got the game in the bag; don't worry about scoring another goal. Don't worry about pretty soccer. *Worry about saving your legs!* If the opportunity presents itself, dump the ball deep into the opponent's end of the field. Let them burn off some of that anger by chasing the ball.

In that same vein, this is not the time to start embarrassing opponents. Don't start nutmegging people and don't get cute playing keep-away. Just bang the ball deep into your opponent's end and wait out the clock. Yeah, it's a cruddy way to finish out the game, but at least you get to go home in one piece.

Note for Coaches – We've all had games like this and we go bananas because we don't feel the officials are doing a good enough job of protecting our players. This is a topic where your time is better spent preparing for the situation than reacting to it. Don't let your players learn this lesson the hard way.

48

DRY BOOTS, HAPPY FEET

Not many things are less enjoyable than putting on a pair of wet soccer shoes. In addition to being uncomfortable, wet boots are heavier than dry ones so they'll slow you down. They can also lead to blisters. Plus they stink. Here's a quick way to turn wet boots into dry boots.

Get some newspaper, ball up one page at a time, and stuff the paper wads into your shoes. It's that simple. The newspaper will absorb the water and the inside of your shoes will be dry by the next morning. Just make sure that you use regular newspaper, not the glossy kind, and that you stuff the balls of paper pretty snuggly into your shoes.

Remember, dry boots means happy feet.

Note for Coaches: You can probably score some easy points with parents by passing this tip along.

49

A FEW MORE THINGS ABOUT RECRUITING

The first volume of *Soccer iQ* includes a chapter on recruiting that I sincerely believe is worth the price of the book in and of itself. However, it occurred to me that I overlooked a few helpful tips, so I'll share them with you now.

If you haven't gotten the memo on this one, recruiting for females has gotten very young. The big schools are spending the bulk of their recruiting efforts on players who are high school sophomores. A great many of the players who commit to these schools are doing so by Christmas break of their junior year. Plenty are committing as sophomores. If you're a girl who wants a look from a BCS school, get on its radar immediately after your freshman year.

Yes, it is a fantastic idea to send the schedule of your upcoming showcase matches to the coaches who you want to watch you play. However, send that schedule at least ten days before the showcase begins, sooner if at all possible. Recruiting travel eats up a good chunk of a college coach's budget, so when it comes to these showcases, we don't just wing it. We'll get a couple hundred emails from hopeful prospects in the weeks leading up to an event and every one of them wants us to watch her play. Planning out the logistics takes a lot of work. We map out the players we need to see, the players we want to see, the fields where they will be playing and the times they'll be playing. Our master plan is usually finished two or three days before the event. Once it is finished, it is very difficult to make changes, and we usually don't.

On the first morning of each and every showcase, I'll get an email from a prospect asking me to watch her play. That's like sending out invitations on the day of your wedding. Sometimes I'll even get these emails on the second morning. Either way, it's too late. If you're not already on our matrix, I'm not going to rework the whole itinerary to fit you in. Get this sorted out ahead of time.

If your team passes out a profile book to coaches, make sure the number you wear on the field matches your number in the book. And make sure your email address and graduation year are listed and listed properly. If there's an error in the profile book that cannot be corrected in time for the showcase, whip up an insert that lists the corrections.

When you go on your unofficial visits, for the love of Pete, turn off your ringer and put your phone in your pocket! Better still, leave it in the car! Be a hero; challenge yourself to go six hours without checking your text messages or your insta-twitter-snap-face-vine-gram. Think of it as a chance to travel back in time to the pioneer days of the 1980s when there were no cell phones. Few things are as insulting to a college coach as a recruit checking her phone at lunch. Incidentally, this also a pretty good policy when you start dating someone new, but only if you want a second date.

Speaking of social media... coaches know how to use it too, and you can bet your butt that when the recruiting process begins, we're checking out everything you've put out there for the world to see. A college player represents far more than just herself. Our players represent their teammates, coaches and university. We want to make sure that we only recruit players who represent us well. Believe me, you don't need to announce your every waking thought to the world, particularly if those thoughts can be categorized as obscene or risqué. If you are a social media risk, then you are also a character risk, and that's not the type of person we need in our program.

Your first objective for the recruiting process is to NOT disqualify yourself. When we're trying to decide on one of several prospects for a spot on our roster, players who commit social media suicide make our decisions much easier. I don't know that social media has ever really helped a prospect's cause, but it sure has hurt a bunch of them, so proceed with caution. If you don't want a college coach to see it, then don't post it.

It would also behoove you to remember that in this day and age, everyone has a camera in their pocket. Keep yourself out of environments where your photo would not speak well of you.

In short, when it comes to the recruiting process, present your very best self. Be polite, organized and professional. Remember, you're not just deciding on the college; the college is also deciding on you.

Note for Coaches: You obviously can't control what your teenage players are going to do, but you should set aside a day for a recruiting lecture that will help guide them through the process. I'm amazed at the amount of families who don't begin the process until late in the prospect's junior year. It's heartbreaking to tell them that our roster is already full. When I tell them that we recruit two and three years out, they all say the same thing: *We had no idea. No one ever told us that.* Give your players a fighting chance by arming them with some information.

A FINAL WORD

When I wrote *Soccer iQ*, I did it for primarily selfish reasons… two of them to be precise. First and foremost, *'writing / publishing a book'* has long been a charter member of my bucket list. I wanted to create something that outlived me, and I wanted to make my daughter proud of her daddy. Secondly, I needed to vent. I needed to vent about the mistakes I've been watching soccer players make over and over for the past two decades. I figured if I wrote a book to the current crop of players, they'd be less likely to make those mistakes and I would be less frustrated when I was out watching them play. It cost me roughly $750 to accomplish my objectives. I figured that if I could just come close to making back my money, the project could be classified as a success. I never anticipated the public response to *Soccer iQ!*

To be honest, I never really paid much attention to how the book was selling on Amazon. I knew that it was selling roughly 20 or 30 copies a month. Now numbers like that would probably send John Grisham spiraling into a deep, dark depression, but I was delighted that anyone would spend ten bucks to read something I wrote.

Then, in October, something quite remarkable happened. Dr. Jay Martin, editor of the NSCAA Soccer Journal, named *Soccer iQ* as a Top 5 Book of the Year, and suddenly, everything took flight. On November 18, I decided to check the book's sales rank on Amazon, something I had done only twice in the sixteen months of the book's existence. When I looked at those numbers, I almost passed out! I was stunned to see that *Soccer iQ* had become the best-selling soccer book on Amazon! Wait, what?

What was even more dizzying was seeing who occupied spots two and three: Mia Hamm and Lionel Messi! Yeah, you've probably heard of them. What in the world just happened? I was walking among legends! I clearly wasn't one of them, but holy smokes! Crazy, right?

Yes, it was flattering to have stumbled into such sublime company, but the true impact I've felt has been from the readers who found value in that book and

111

felt connected enough to share their comments with me. Their kind words have given me a sense of fulfillment I had never anticipated. I have been particularly humbled by those coaches who enjoyed *Soccer iQ* enough to order copies for every player on their team. I hope it has served you well!

I've received a lot of wonderful feedback about *Soccer iQ*, but my favorite response came from a men's college coach who simply wrote:

"Dan, what's the quickest way to get 30 copies of your book? I loved the book and need my players to read it ASAP."

Isn't it great when college coaches get all sentimental like that?

Anyway, thanks for reading! This will likely be the final volume of the *Soccer iQ* series. I did my best to put out a product that was every bit as valuable as the first volume. If you're going to pay to read something I've written, then I want to have a clear conscience about it! I hope that, in your eyes, I've reached my objective and you feel like you've gotten your money's worth.

I welcome your feedback. Just send me a note at coach@soccerpoet.com.

I invite you to read my blog at www.soccerpoet.com and to be my Twitter friend: @soccerpoet.

If you feel you've gotten your money's worth from *Soccer iQ Volume 2*, please take 30 seconds to leave me a five-star review on Amazon. That's the best gift you can possibly give an author. Thank you in advance!

Wouldn't it be great if all your teammates read this book? If you'd like to place a bulk order of the paperback version for your organization, please email me at coach@soccerpoet.com. I'll give you a discount!

Keep reading for a sample chapter from my upcoming book, *Everything Your Coach Never Told You Because You're a Girl*.

OTHER BOOKS BY DAN BLANK

Soccer iQ Volume 1 — The Amazon best-seller and an NSCAA Soccer Journal Top 5 Book of the Year. Available in paperback and for Kindle.

HAPPY FEET — How to Be a Gold Star Soccer Parent (Everything the Coach, the Ref and Your Kid Want You to Know) — The best gift you can give a soccer parent! This book includes free companion videos to explain some of soccer's more mysterious concepts such as the advantage rule, offside, soccer systems and combination play. It also explains the most common errors that well-meaning soccer parents make without even realizing it.

Everything Your Coach Never Told You Because You're a Girl — This is what your coaches would have said to you if you were a boy, told through the story of a small college team that won more games than it ever had a right to win. It's a straightforward look at the qualities that define the most competitive females. Available in 2014.

ROOKIE — Surviving Your Freshman Year of College Soccer — A survival guide for those about to face the rigors of college soccer. Available in 2014.

21

GO FOR THE CUT

"The object of war is not to die for your country; it's to make the other guy die for his." - General George S. Patton

What we do is not about making friends. It's about conquest.

I remember being eight years old, watching a Saturday afternoon boxing match on the television with my dad. One of the boxers sustained a cut above his eye and blood was streaming down his face. Immediately his opponent began aiming every punch at that cut, and I couldn't understand why. It went against everything I had learned in school, particularly that you help someone who is hurt. In my mind, the other boxer should have started aiming somewhere else. I was very confused.

"Why does he keep hitting that man's cut," I asked my father.

My dad laughed for a second. He realized that I hadn't learned one of the principles of boxing. He explained that when you cut your opponent, you aim for that cut because you have a chance to end the fight. In other words, when you find a weakness, you need to exploit it. This is not a principle limited to boxing.

As long as there have been sports there have been coaches struggling to get their players to realize that when you get an opponent vulnerable, you've got to shift into a higher gear and go for the kill. In boxing this principle is easy to observe because it is virtually literal. In other competitions it might not be so obvious.

In 2000 our team had reached the point where we actually had the chance to lead some games. Our inability to finish off our opponents became a major issue for us. As a program starved for wins, it was very frustrating to get the upper hand on a team only to have that team come back to tie the game and eventually win it. We were like the boxer who opens a cut over the opponent's eye and then starts aiming for his shoulders. We didn't recognize those moments when an opponent was vulnerable, so we couldn't exploit them.

My players were still maturing as competitors. They kept stepping out of character at the wrong time, like, while the game was still in progress. Regardless of the frenzy with which they began a game, if we took the lead, they became satisfied. Satisfied people are nice people. We didn't need nice people. I needed the players to understand that there are no points for nice. There are only points for points.

We needed to stop thinking in terms of the scoreboard and to start thinking in terms of the opponent's spirit. Scoring the first goal equates to winning a battle; that's great, but it's very small-picture. The big picture is the crack it puts into the foundation of a team's spirit. That's where the first goal cuts the opponent – in its spirit. If you can knock out a team's spirit, that team loses its will to fight. The sooner you can shatter your opponent's will, the more likely you are to win.

In soccer and many other sports, the spirit-goal relationship is cyclical. You score a goal; you damage the spirit, which should make it easier to score the next goal – which further damages the spirit. Eventually the spirit breaks and that's when the proverbial floodgates open. The key is recognizing when a spirit has become vulnerable and then refusing to give it the chance to heal. When a boxer staggers his opponent, he immediately shifts into a higher gear and begins to fight with much more urgency. He knows that if the injured opponent can hang on until the end of the round, he'll have a chance to heal. So the boxer steps up his tempo and tries to end the fight before the round expires.

I begged the players, particularly our captain Joelle, that the next time we took a lead, we needed to try and end the game right then and there. We needed to smell blood and go in for the kill. If we could break our opponent's spirit, that team wouldn't have the will to stage a comeback.

Our next game was against a team that we had tied once and lost to five times in the first three years of our program's existence. But with each passing defeat, we had inched a little closer to them. By 2000 we had narrowed the talent gap to a manageable margin. Now, on a beautiful October night, Joelle opened the scoring and we had finally taken a lead on our nemesis.

When we got that first goal, Joelle's teammates mobbed her in celebration, but Joelle was having none of it! She shoved them away and immediately began campaigning for more urgency. She was jabbing her finger toward her teammates and saying, "We're not done! We finish this team right now!" Joelle was tired of heartbreaking losses. She wanted to eliminate that possibility entirely. She wasn't going to let her teammates forget the story I had told them about the cut boxer. Joelle wanted to break spirits and she got her teammates to climb on board. Instead of going from angry to satisfied, we went from angry to enraged. We saw a cut and we began aiming for it with everything we had.

In an amazing display of going for the cut, we scored four more goals in the next eleven minutes to put the game out of reach by half-time. The opponent may as well have sent cardboard cutouts to play the second half. We had scored a first-half knockout. The fight had ended before the first half was over because we recognized a vulnerability and we chose to bombard it. Joelle's goal had won us momentum, and momentum must breed urgency.

There is a saying that a 2-0 lead is the most dangerous lead in soccer. To the average competitor, it may be. For the average competitor, whose effort is a reflection of the scoreboard, a 2-0 lead is often a case of 'next goal wins.' If the trailing team cuts the lead to 2-1, there is often a huge swing in momentum and it isn't uncommon for them to go on and win the game 3-2.

Winners have no issues with a two-goal lead. As a matter of fact, winners love a two-goal lead! Winners recognize a two-goal lead as a bridge to a three-goal lead, and then a four-goal lead, and so on. Winners play with an unbridled urgency to break spirits. That urgency stays with them regardless of what the scoreboard says. When human nature tells us we can ease up, winners instead kick into a higher gear. They don't care if they are winning by two or twelve, that urgency stays with them. If your team is giving away two-goal leads, you have an unacceptable competitive problem because you are measuring your effort against the scoreboard. And that will always spell disaster.

Winners recognize the chance to break spirits, and they don't let those chances pass quietly. When they see a chance to put the game out of reach, they respond with frenetic urgency. The spirit is the head of the opponent. If you chop off the head, the body will follow – and the game is yours.

You made the decision to go all in; now the opportunity to slam the door is upon you. Once you break an opponent's spirit, she is at your mercy. Do not give her the opportunity to heal her spirit before the result is out of reach. Finish her!

Believe me when I tell you, when the opponent bleeds, go for the cut.

ABOUT THE AUTHOR

Dan Blank is the author of the Amazon bestseller, *Soccer iQ*, and has been coaching college soccer for over twenty years. He is the first coach in Southeastern Conference history to lead the conference's best defense in consecutive years at different universities (Ole Miss 2009, Georgia 2010). He has an 'A' License from the USSF and an Advanced National Diploma from the NSCAA. You can buy his books and read his blog at www.soccerpoet.com.

Made in the USA
San Bernardino, CA
21 June 2016